W9-BKC-263

THERAPY?

JOYCE HOUSER WARD, M.F.C.T.

Wynwood® Press
Tarrytown, New York

Library of Congress Cataloging-in-Publication Data

Ward, Joyce Houser.
Therapy? : unmasking the fears, shattering the myths, finding the path to wellness / Joyce Houser Ward. — 1st ed.
p. cm.
ISBN 0-922066-75-2
1. Psychotherapy—Popular works. 2. Psychotherapy —Case studies.
I. Title.
RC480.515.W37 1992 91-30411
616.89'14—dc20 CIP

Published by Wynwood® Press
Tarrytown, New York
An Imprint of Gleneida Publishing Group
Printed in the United States of America

To anyone who has the courage to hope
and the willingness to work toward
emotional and spiritual healing

CONTENTS

ACKNOWLEDGMENTS

Thanks to Paul, my father, for always believing in me and encouraging me to write.

Thanks to Lilian, my mother, for having a loving heart and a mind open to hearing the truth.

Thanks to Jerry, my brother, for being there, caring so much, and for your special sense of humor.

Thanks to Arian, my love, my husband, for all the ways you sustain me, and for your commitment to our life together.

Thanks to my family, and wonderful friends, for your consistent support, understanding, and love.

Thanks to Joan Follendore, for being more than a great editor and agent—for being a patient teacher, and real friend.

Thanks to Stephan Tobin, for showing me, by example, what it means to be a good therapist.

Thanks to all my clients, for giving me so much of yourselves in our work together.

Thanks to the 12-Step Program, for providing spiritual direction, a structure for recovery, and unconditional acceptance.

Thanks to the brilliant authors, whose writing contributed to this book and to my life.

Thanks to God, for leading me in the direction I need to go, and for always staying with me, even when I forget You.

Grateful acknowledgment is given for permission to reprint the following:

Pp. 58, 140, 175, 184: Excerpts from ADDICTION AND GRACE by Gerald G. May. Copyright © 1988 by Gerald G. May. Reprinted by permission of HarperCollins, publishers. *P. 29:* From W. H. AUDEN: COLLECTED POEMS by W. H. Auden, ed. by Edward Mendelson. Copyright © 1975 by Edward Mendelson. William Meredith & Monroe K. Spears, Executors of the Estate of W. H. Auden. Reprinted by permission of Random House, Inc. *Pp. 151, 157–158, 167:* Excerpts from BETWEEN THERAPIST AND CLIENT by Michael Kahn (W. H. Freeman and Co., 1991). *Pp. 49, 59, 103:* From THE DRAMA OF THE GIFTED CHILD by Alice Miller (New York: Basic Books, 1981). *Pp. 11, 128, 170:* Excerpts from "Little Gidding" and "East Coker" in FOUR QUARTETS, copyright 1932 by T.S. Eliot and renewed 1971 by Esme Valerie Eliot. Reprinted by permission of Harcourt Brace Jovanovich, Inc. *Pp. 93, 98–99, 132*: Reprinted with the permission of the publishers Health Communications, Inc., Deerfield Beach, Florida, from HEALING THE SHAME THAT BINDS YOU, by John Bradshaw, copyright date 1990. *P. 89:* Excerpts from LEAVING THE ENCHANTED FOREST by Stephanie Covington and Liana Beckett. Copyright 1988 by Stephanie Covington and Liana Beckett. Reprinted by permission of HarperCollins, publishers. *Pp. 25, 38, 79, 169, 181–182:* From THE ROAD LESS TRAVELED, copyright 1978 by M. Scott Peck, M.D. Reprinted by permission of Simon & Schuster, Inc. *Pp. 60, 123–124, 161, 182:* Excerpts from SOULMAKING by Alan Jones. Copyright 1985 by Alan Jones. Reprinted by permission of HarperCollins, publishers. *P. 136:* Excerpt from STAGE II RECOVERY by Earnie Larsen. Copyright 1985 by Earnie Larsen. Reprinted by permission of HarperCollins, publishers. *P. 54:* SURPLUS POWERLESSNESS, by Michael Lerner, copyright 1986 by Michael Lerner. Available through TIKKUN Magazine, 5100 Leona St., Oakland, CA 94619. *P. 34:* From THOU SHALT NOT BE AWARE, by Alice Miller. Copyright 1984 by Alice Miller. Reprinted by permission of Farrar, Straus and Giroux, Inc. *Pp. 137, 147:* From WITNESS TO THE FIRE by Linda Schierse Leonard, © 1989. Reprinted by arrangement with Shambhala Publications, Inc. 300 Massachusetts Ave., Boston, MA 02115.

To arrive where you are, to get from where you are not,
You must go by a way wherein there is no ecstasy.
. . . And what you do not know is the only thing you know. . . .

—T. S. Eliot
"East Coker"
Four Quartets

INTRODUCTION

Self-help isn't enough when you're hurting emotionally, trying and trying to find your way out, but feeling "stuck" or like you're going in circles. Some problems just can't be solved alone, they need a professional's help.

We all like to believe we can manage our lives, achieve our goals, and be relatively happy. When emotional problems arise, we want to solve them quickly and independently—and often we can. But just when we think we've finally resolved some predicament forever, it recurs, revealing a pattern. These "stuck" times may seem hopeless, but that doesn't mean they are. They are simply indicators that it's time to see a therapist.

Randy came to me feeling desperate. "I've read at least ten books on relationships," he said, "but I'm still going after women who aren't right for me. Everything starts out great and I get my hopes up, because it looks like this time it's different; this time it's real. Then somehow things take a turn, and begin to fall apart—it may last a month or a year, but they all end the same. I can't keep doing this. It hurts too much."

Randy needed more than insights gained through reading to change his choices and actions in relationships, and to heal the still prevalent pain from his past, the underlying cause of this frustrating and disappointing pattern.

There are many approaches to healing emotional pain. Psychotherapy is one of them, and there are many approaches to therapy. My purpose here is not to explain, define, or defend the various forms of therapy available. Rather, my purpose is to encourage and support you in your decision to change, and to prepare you for what you may experience. I personally believe in a therapeutic process that allows for exploration of the past to help clarify and heal the present. True, you can't change the events of the past, but you *can* change the present by integrating the past—feeling it, expressing it, and understanding its effects.

I believe that without uncovering and healing the deepest sources of pain, change is only superficial.

In this book I will tell you stories of people I have worked with—what they went through when they first realized they needed help, what they experienced when they began therapy, and what the process was like for them, step by step. The names have been changed and the facts altered where needed, to guarantee the clients' confidentiality.

Maybe you're considering psychotherapy, or maybe someone who cares about you has suggested you try it. You're probably feeling uneasy and have a lot of questions and doubts. Or perhaps you've already begun therapy, but the process is different from what you expected, and you're concerned.

Every person's experience is unique, of course—so no full description of what will happen to you can be given beforehand. However, there are some commonalities. Part of what makes entering therapy frightening is that so little is written about what to expect. Yes, it can be a fearful process, but it's also exciting and rewarding.

The good news is that you can feel better. The bad news is that you probably have to feel worse first, as you face and embrace your feelings. The human instinct to run is natural, but you must do the opposite. Your hesitancy is natural, too, and understandable. But the cost of living defensively is a loss of self. I believe the cost is too high.

It saddens me to see people living with emotional pain—chronic depression, anxiety, disappointment, guilt, rage—and never doing anything about it. Why don't they, when so much help is available? Every area of their lives is affected: health, relationships, work, finances. Everyone has his or her own answers to the question, Why not? But, underneath all those answers lie shame, fear, and lack of information.

My client Carrie struggled with shame, saying, "I looked at your phone number for months before gathering the courage to call. I thought calling a therapist meant I was sick or crazy, and I didn't want to see myself like that."

Although more and more people enter therapy every year, Carrie knew no one personally who had been through it. She continued, "I couldn't talk to anyone about my decision, and that made it worse." Her isolation created more feelings of shame, because she thought the people around her wouldn't understand. She lacked self-confidence, and she lacked support.

Fear of being labeled "sick" or "crazy" unfortunately keeps many people from getting help. Anyone who labels people shows a lack of insight, compassion, and knowledge. The truth is, we all have problems, and there's no clear line dividing wellness from illness. Emotional health is a continuum, and where we are on that continuum fluctuates throughout our lifetime.

When friends or relatives tell me again and again about the same problems, but never seek help to solve them, I feel as if we're standing together outside a locked door. On the other side of the door is a room full of life's treasures, fulfillments, and freedoms. The key to the door is about a mile away, and I tell the person where to find it. What happens next always surprises me. The person says, "No, there's really no key there," or, "A mile is just too far to walk," or, "There's nothing on the other side of the door anyway." Ignorance, fear, and shame have closed their minds.

While more vague and hidden than physical pain, emotional pain can hurt just as badly. When ignored, it can also become physical—body aches and stress-related illnesses. Pain can express itself through compulsive and impulsive actions. It may thwart action through procrastination, indecisiveness, or lack of motivation.

We instinctively run from pain, or try to stop it. However, feelings do need to be felt and expressed, if not immediately then eventually. Current situations can cause emotional pain, but often thoughts, feelings, and memories are *triggered* in the present while having their roots in the past, even the distant past. Pervasive unhappiness usually points to something hidden and unresolved. Avoidance works for the moment, but it is not a solution. In fact, avoidance prolongs and distorts pain, preventing healing. A defensive lifestyle becomes a liability more than a protection. Ironically, healing is contained *within* those painful thoughts, feelings, and memories that we struggle so hard to deny.

If you have lived with unresolved emotional pain and problems for a long time, by now you may feel heartsick—as if your entire "being" hurts—either acutely, or in a dull, nagging way. You don't know why, but you know something is wrong. You may see the effects of the inner turmoil on your relationships, your health, or your work. Finally, you are acknowledging your unhappiness, wondering how you can change, and beginning to seek a solution. This is the turning point in your emotional growth, sometimes referred to as "hitting bottom." The despair that you feel is crucial. It leads you to surrender to the need for help.

In my practice, I see the miracle that occurs when painful feelings are acknowledged and expressed in the presence of an understanding, caring, trained listener. I also see the intense fear, shame, and confusion in the initial stages of reaching out, accompanying the first opening-up to hidden feelings.

It's natural to fear the unknown—it means giving up control, being vulnerable, and feeling pain. It takes a lot of courage to really face yourself, admit problems, and be open to change. Your questions and doubts may sound like this:

"*Do I really need it*?" The fact that you're considering getting help means something is bothering you that you aren't able to resolve alone. Admitting to yourself that there's a problem may be difficult, admitting this to another person, more difficult still. However, personal growth is a choice that no one can make for you. Without growth, the best you can expect is to stay as you are.

"*You can't trust others, anyway.*" You might have been taught that strength means self-reliance, or handling it alone. There's no disgrace in asking for help; you're fortunate that help is available and that there is a choice of sources. Your fears and mistrust are normal aspects of the problems you're seeking to solve. For now, you'll have to act courageously, despite those fears, in order to take the first step.

"*Why can't I just talk to a friend?*" Chances are you already have. Friends are especially valuable, but sometimes they aren't enough. Healing professionals bring study, experience, and more objectivity to your interactions.

"*It probably won't help anyway.*" Cynicism is just a cover-up for fear of taking a chance. Of course, not all problems can be solved through therapy, but many can.

"*But I don't want to spend all that time and money!*" Of course you don't. Everyone wishes for instant cures; as a matter of fact, an isolated crisis can be worked through in a relatively short period of time. Problems that have been around for a long time require more effort.

The process of therapy is strange and uncomfortable in the beginning; it's natural to feel disoriented and anxious at first. Many ask, "Where do I start?" Start where you are, and the rest will unfold. You and your therapist will learn about you together. Therapy is a kind of psychic renovation process in which old, conditioned, automatic, defensive habits are carefully exposed and peeled away. Feelings and memories—suppressed sometimes for years—are unearthed and brought to light. The energy of these feelings can be immense; sometimes, especially at first, they are painful and frightening. The more powerful the feeling, the stronger the defense has been against it.

Each feeling has a story behind it needing to be told, to be brought to consciousness. However, the upset created by its emergence is often threatening and overwhelming. In the middle of that upset, I hear clients in anguish ask about what's happening to them, and how to handle it. They say:

"I feel like I'm going to fall apart, go crazy . . . maybe I won't be able to work, and then what?"

"I'm afraid if I start crying, I'll never stop. . . ."

"If I really let go and get angry, maybe I'll destroy things or hurt someone, and then I'll be sorry."

"Maybe I'm going to die. The feelings are so big, they'll kill me. I won't make it through."

Because I experienced some of these fears and doubts when I began my own therapy, I know how they feel. In time, I learned how to "feel the fear and do it anyway." I learned that risk and doubt are parts of growing, and that whatever happens is usually different from what we fear will happen.

Have hope and know that many others have gone before you and will go after you as well. Let this book accompany you through the therapy process. It will be a reminder that you're not alone, and it will be a source of encouragement if you lose heart.

Joyce Houser Ward
Santa Monica, CA

THERAPY?

CHAPTER 1

FACING THE UNKNOWN: FIRST STEPS INTO THERAPY

It takes courage to change. Talking about it is easy, but at the moment of truth, when it's time to take action, something happens—you falter, pull back, get scared. Frustrating, isn't it? To change the course of your life, you have to be willing to step over the edge of the familiar, into the unknown. Therapy is a walk into the unknown, led by the therapist who is your experienced and supportive guide. The walk holds great promise, but the first step—making the decision to begin—is up to you. When you consider making that move, you may discover just how rooted, how "set in your ways" you are. People get stuck in ruts—comfortable in themselves, their lives, and their problems.

What is it that stops action? What allows people to complain a lot, and even to discuss alternatives, but never make a move? One answer is fear—the fear of risk. Whether you like where you are or not, it's what you're used to, and therefore predictable and safe. Taking a risk means choosing to change, not knowing the result in advance, or how you will feel about it. There's no guarantee that the outcome will be favorable, or one that you planned. And to make matters worse, once a decision is put into action, you generally can't go back to the old ways. So you're destined to follow through, carried along by a momentum of your own making, whether you like it or not. No wonder you resist! It's natural. Having the courage to change is having the courage not just to face the uncertainty of the unknown, but also to accept responsibility for the decision.

Some of my clients, even after deciding to begin therapy, struggle for many weeks to continue with it. One man, Gene, wondered aloud, "What am I doing here? What if this doesn't work and I'm wasting my time and money? How can I get into this when I don't know for sure what will happen to me?"

I understood Gene's concern and reluctance. Even though I couldn't give him a guarantee, I told him I had worked with many people and had seen their lives change, as mine had changed through my own therapy. I knew Gene was upset because he couldn't calculate his progress right away, so I told him, "Therapy is a subtle and complex process. You can't measure results clearly and simply, from the first day, as you could if you were building a house. Although you don't see it now, and you're uncomfortable taking chances, suddenly you will feel better, and your time and money will have been well invested. You'll look forward to coming here, and you'll know you've made the right decision."

Even some people who love taking chances, and seek them out, have their limits. A person who is daring in one aspect of life may be timid in another. For example, someone who chooses to sky-dive may embrace the thrill of physical risk, but may shy away from emotional risk in intimate relationships.

Most people are upset by feeling too out of control; many never take risks voluntarily. Their lives are devoted to maintaining the safety of the status quo. This adherence to the familiar is often a reaction to a tumultuous or unpredictable early life, perhaps from an emotionally unstable family. Chaos is terrifying for children, so they respond by trying to control whatever they can—their own emotions, their bodies, their surroundings.

Since childhood, Gene had been frightened by change. He grew up with a father who frequently started arguments, and then left the house, slamming the door behind him. No one knew when his father would be back—maybe late that night, maybe not until the next day. Gene's mother would withdraw into depression and drinking when her husband left, occasionally venting her suppressed rage on those around her.

Gene used self-control to cope with the chaos. He said, "I used to do the same thing every time Dad left. I'd go to my room and start building something out of wooden blocks—one, two, three, four, five . . . I counted the blocks up to ten, as I placed them, and then started counting over again. I told myself that by the time I finished, Dad would be home. Sometimes it worked and he'd come home while I was still building. Other times I just went to sleep, because I couldn't stay awake any longer." Children think magically. Gene thought that by ordering the little world of his room he could bring his father back, and restore order and safety to the family.

In later life the traumatized adult may continue to try to avoid change, in order to preserve inner security. Of course, no one can avoid change. Life changes us whether we welcome it or fight it. The reluctant individual will try to adjust or cope as quickly as possible, to minimize upset. Unfortunately, what is missed in this passive acceptance of change is the joy and power of responsibility. When we *choose* to change, we are creating our "selves," joining forces with life to change in a particular direction. There is a thrill and a satisfaction in this action, even if the result is failure. We learn from failure how to achieve success, and regardless of the results, we have taken a stand.

Responsibility is a paradox. It can be seen as both a burden and a freedom. Either way, there's no avoiding it. *The person who attempts to avoid responsibility for change by making no decisions is indirectly deciding to stay the same.*

Some people hope for change—hope that life will change their circumstances, do it for them. They sit back and wait for it to happen, so they don't have to do it themselves. Life does bring change, but not necessarily the way they hope.

Other people sincerely want a change but believe it's impossible, at least impossible *for them.* They feel powerless, trapped, and resigned. People with this negative belief are stuck in an illusion they perpetuate.

It's true that not all obstacles are surmountable, but negative beliefs can severely limit growth. There's no confidence in self, no faith in God or life. This pessimism often comes from a family in which the parents had little hope, where everyone was a victim, and nothing was possible, or where parents were critical or derogatory.

Philip and Barbara came to see me because they felt hopeless in their marriage. It was immediately evident that nothing dynamic was going on between them. They were both restrained, polite, and depressed. As they discovered attitudes toward their relationship that were previously unexamined, Barbara remembered her mother's discouraging platitudes: "If you don't expect anything, you won't be disappointed." "Men are all alike." "It has always been this way, and it will always be this way."

No matter what your feelings and beliefs are about change, it's unavoidable. And if you would like to *participate in directing your life,* you will have to accept the challenge of risk.

Psychotherapy is a way to facilitate change in your life, but making the decision to begin requires the kind of courage and faith you may feel you lack. Many people read about therapy, talk to friends about it, and consider it for months or even years before actually making a commitment to it. Others take the initial steps and begin, but then quickly back out. Therapy challenges the individual to face the unknown of the inner self, in a way that most people never considered or even knew possible. As the process continues, it becomes apparent that their unknown, inner region is vast and deep. It contains truths that have been hidden and are often hard to acknowledge. It evokes intense, and sometimes threatening, feelings.

In *The Road Less Traveled*, M. Scott Peck, M.D., has this to say:

> Entering psychotherapy is an act of the greatest courage. The primary reason people do not undergo psychotherapy is not that they lack the money but that they lack the courage. It is because they possess this courage, on the other hand, that many psychoanalytic patients, even at the outset of therapy and contrary to their stereotypical image, are people who are basically much stronger and healthier than average.

To have courage doesn't mean to be fearless but rather to take action in spite of being afraid. Often people begin psychotherapy hoping the experience will be a quick fix. The unspoken (or sometimes spoken) wish is for a prescription—an insight or a formula for action—to solve their problems.

The truth is that the therapist is not a problem-solver, but a guide into the inner world of thoughts, feelings, and memories. This comes as a shock to most people, and sometimes a disappointment.

"You mean I have to do this myself?" The answer is, Yes. The therapist has the map, but you have to take the trip. The route differs with each individual. What is the same for all, however, is facing the unknown; and what is shaken is no less than our identities.

We all have an image of ourselves. Self-image is complex, variable, and sometimes even vague, but we do identify ourselves with certain characteristics. Therapy throws this self-image into question. It challenges taken-for-granted beliefs. It reveals why we behave in certain ways, and examines our previously unexamined decisions to stay the same.

To illustrate: A woman name Cynthia began therapy with me to help her through the pain of divorce. Three months prior she had moved out of the house where she lived with her husband. She said she knew the marriage was wrong for her and she wanted to get on with her life. She couldn't understand why she still cried at night, and hadn't gotten over it. Cynthia's self-image was one of strength, confidence, and efficiency—all positive attributes.

As we began to work together, I learned she had left other relationships with the same fortitude and certainty of purpose. "Why waste time?" was her attitude. "It would be weak and masochistic to stay in a situation that's painful." On the surface, she was a very optimistic, self-affirming woman. But as we looked further into her past, Cynthia revealed she had left home at age fifteen because her family life was "too painful," and she "never looked back." She took care of herself from then on, and was proud of it.

While this strategy had worked for Cynthia, something was missing. In order to survive the neglect and abuse of her parents, she made a decision to need no one, to "move on"—away from the pain. With this pattern established, whenever things got rough in a relationship she simply got out. In effect, she cut herself off from all deep feelings in relationships, in order not to be vulnerable, and to protect herself from being hurt again.

This last time, however, was different; it didn't work. She was tired of running and tired of feeling nothing. The disappointment of her losses caught up with her. She couldn't stop crying and didn't know why. She felt weak, ashamed, confused.

The reasons for Cynthia's pain came pouring out. Long-buried feelings of hurt, despair, and anger at her childhood circumstances began to surface. As the truth appeared to Cynthia, she became more and more agitated. Along with the pain of her feelings, her confident, strong self-image was threatened. She realized that the cost of maintaining invulnerable self-sufficiency was too high. All her adult life she was proud of her strength. Now she saw it in a different light. She saw that what she had called strength was actually a defense against hurt.

She wondered whether she had given up her relationships too soon. And what if that were true? What was she supposed to do about it? Her self-esteem was built around this willful, fast-moving personality she had developed. Her confidence was based on her ability to stay in control no matter what. Who would Cynthia be if she changed? She feared she would become someone that neither she nor anyone else could respect. She was afraid to let in feelings and get closer to people; that meant being vulnerable, weak, and a victim of others. Her proud self-image would be lost.

This initial upset was only the beginning for Cynthia, and it all came as a big surprise. She had come to me seeking help to get over her divorce as quickly as possible. What she found instead was her unknown self. Her personal unknown was the world of deep feelings in intimate relationships. Cynthia had been living a life of emotional deprivation, begun in her childhood through her parents' neglect. In her adult life, she perpetuated the deprivation by never allowing herself to be really close to anyone, not even her husband. To avoid pain, she robbed herself of love.

Cynthia had to find the courage to face the truth about herself and feel the pain not only of her childhood but of what she missed in her adult life. Instead of being tough and controlled, in therapy she would have to let down her guard and open up to the grief inside. She previously saw vulnerability only as a weakness. Now Cynthia realized a paradox—it takes great strength to be vulnerable, to relinquish control and allow the painful healing process to take place.

This was another challenge to Cynthia's cherished self-image.

She was at a crossroads. She could continue on her old familiar path, nonthreatening and nonsatisfying, or she could go in a new direction with the promise of more emotional fulfillment.

Taking a new path meant shedding some of her old identity. "Who will I be?" Cynthia asked. "And what guarantee do I have that I'll get what I want once I change?"

"There are no guarantees," I answered. "I wish there were. Everyone would have it easier that way. And 'Who will I be?' is unanswerable right now, too. Just as a caterpillar when building its cocoon doesn't know it will become a butterfly, you can't know your transformation until you experience it. Going into the cocoon is an act of faith. What have you got to lose?"

"Everything!" she cried.

"So it seems," I said, "but you won't. You'll lose some negative behaviors, and what you gain will be positive. You're attached to the old ways because they helped you survive and made you feel safe, but they also caused you pain, and blocked happiness."

Identity is something so intangible and so close to us that we don't see it, we just take it for granted. Seeing your own identity is like trying to see your face without a mirror. Introspection is threatening because it questions what seems so essential and basic to who we are. We're used to holding tightly to concepts of ourselves. When we challenge those beliefs, we encounter a lot of resistance.

How many times have you heard it said, "People don't change"? That belief is a defense and a trap, keeping us stuck where we are. People *do* change. Circumstances and experience change people, sometimes for better and sometimes for worse. However, for change to occur in a less random manner, in harmony with our values and wishes, we have to participate in, and direct, the change process. We must become conscious of our problems, define the ways we want to change, and commit ourselves to the work required to bring about the desired results. The work requires stepping into the unknown, which is painful.

As we change—as we dare to or are forced to—we are temporarily faced with a void, an uncertainty. This is a transition period that can be extremely uncomfortable. It feels as if one's body, mind, and soul are being stretched in all directions while going nowhere. This transition feels like walking in the dark, blind and fumbling. You want desperately to push for a solution, but there is none yet.

There are other situations that evoke this type of discomfort to a lesser degree, like starting a new job, or entering a social group without knowing anyone.

From time to time during this stressful and confusing transition, Cynthia felt like giving up, quitting. "What's the point of all this?" she'd ask. "I feel worse than when I started. At least then I knew who I was."

In the midst of this angst, one is constantly pulled back to the old ways. Wouldn't it be easier to give up the struggle and go back to the familiar? It's tempting. And many people do give up. They start enthusiastically, only to bail out when it gets rough. Any process involving letting go of something, or building something new, takes determination and tenacity.

W. H. Auden wrote, in his poem "Age of Anxiety":

We would rather be ruined than changed
We would rather die in our dread
Than climb the cross of the moment
And let our illusions die.

Any change involves loss, and loss is very often painful. When we leave something behind—a house, a job, a lover, a city, an addiction, or an aspect of our self-image—there is almost always some sadness involved.

The change may be welcome, but the house, job, or lover left behind wasn't all bad. So while we might be glad to give up some aspects, we cling to the ones that made us happy. Anything we depended on in the past offered something—some meaning, connection, safety, or refuge—even if minimal.

You might ask, "What could possibly be sad about letting go of alcoholism or an abusive relationship?"

For an alcoholic, drinking is a reliable source of comfort, "high," or escape, and, unlike dealings with people, a "friendship" with alcohol doesn't seem, to the alcoholic, to require compromise. Of course, eventually the "friend" becomes an enemy, potentially causing loss of health, family, respect, often loss of job and all security. Nevertheless, when the addiction is relinquished, a great void remains which requires a total change in lifestyle and behavior, to fill. Therapy provides support in the processes of letting go of the old and constructing the new.

Grieving for what is lost in the change is a difficult part of growing, but a vital one. When past losses and disappointments have been especially crushing or numerous, experiencing more pain seems intolerable. It isn't. Slowly, and with help, you work through it, and reach a new beginning.

Letting go of alcohol was especially difficult for Barry, an acquaintance of mine. He learned to drink at home with his father, Gil, a boisterous, fun-loving man who, according to Barry, "worked hard and drank hard." Gil taught Barry a lot of things, and Barry loved and admired his father. When Barry became a young adult, he and Gil often went to bars together. Occasionally, Gil would get so drunk he'd curse and insult people in the bar.

"Where was your mother in all this?" I asked.

"Oh, she stayed home," he answered. "She was always depressed and tired."

At the time, no one seemed to think there was a problem, least of all Barry. However, years later, Barry's life was full of problems. When I met him, he was in Alcoholics Anonymous, and had been sober for four years. He told me the story:

> At twenty two, I married a woman I met in a bar. We loved to "party" together—in fact our relationship was based on it—drinking and sex. It took some time before the party degenerated into cheating, lying, and other abuse. It got so sick and ugly, and finally ended when I caught her with another man. I think she really wanted me to find her with him, so we could both get out.
>
> When I left her, I was miserable, and went downhill fast, drinking. I lost my job, hated myself. Then I went to see a therapist who took one look at me and suggested an A.A. meeting.
>
> Of course, I didn't think of myself as an alcoholic, but I was desperate, so I went to A.A., and therapy. I realized not only was I an alcoholic, but so was my ex-wife, and so was my father!

What Barry discovered was that the ritual of drinking had been woven into the fabric of his relationship with his father. Drinking, he had been taught, was part of being a man, and part of love. The threads of his father's love for him, and his love for his father, were crisscrossed and tangled with the ever-present thread of alcohol. No wonder he married a woman who drank; it was a familiar relationship.

Barry continued:

> I finally realized what drinking meant to me—it was part of my masculinity, and my only link to intimacy with other people. How could I give that up? No way did I want to, but in therapy and A.A., it began to dawn on me that I had to do it. I saw that drinking actually got in the way. My father's addiction just hid his true feelings, and I was doing the same. Being a drunk did not make me a man. And the relationships I'd experienced with

> my parents and ex-wife were just shadows of real intimacy.
>
> I'd always loved my parents, and thought my father was great, especially compared to my mother, who was so silent and withdrawn. But now I see that drinking also keeps people at a distance. They were both in pain and didn't know how to be close to each other. So I didn't get much of what I really needed from either of them. What I did get from Dad I cherished, but it had booze written all over it. To get his love, I had to drink, too. Quitting felt like losing the only thing I ever could count on. And I felt I was losing my link to my family. The separation was so painful, but I had to let go of the bottle if I wanted to grow, if I ever wanted to find out what was possible for me.

There are those for whom the pain of growth feels insurmountable: They close their hearts forever. Hardened hearts and rigid minds are evident all around us. The decision to shut down and retreat from emotional vulnerability is often made at an early age, attempting protection against further losses. *But to heal loss, we must feel loss.*

By retreating from risk of loss, the illusion of safety is created. While a retreat appears to ward off danger, it creates new problems—loneliness, limitations, and the fears accompanying isolation. We can run but we can't hide, it is said. We can never truly hide from life. Accepting the risk of living and choosing to grow is not easy. Facing the unknown requires a leap of faith. "Faith in what?" you may ask.

One answer to that is to have faith in the healing process of nature (some call that nature *God*). Healing *does* happen, and when it does, the need to live defensively is lessened.

Another answer is having faith in yourself. You wouldn't be asking the questions if you weren't prepared to hear the answers and to do your share of the work. You can "pray as if it all depends on God, but work as if it all depends on you."

Finally, have faith in your therapist—to guide and support you.

"But how do I choose a therapist?" you ask. "How do I know who to trust?" These are very good questions, and they deserve a thorough reply.

There are many therapists and types of therapy around these days. The thought of having to choose one is enough to make some people give up before they begin. Television and movies don't help, as they usually portray unappealing stereotypes: the outdated image of the cold, authoritarian male peering over his desk; the more modern (but equally discouraging), sentimental, simpleton pal/shrink, feigning empathy and sincerity; the detached money-grubber who couldn't care less about the client; the unethical one who takes sexual advantage in the name of treatment. Needless to say, there are those who are rigid, ineffective or inappropriate, mawkish or greedy. But there are also those who are committed, ethical, and expert, and who care about their clients.

So how do you choose? I advise using a combination of information and intuition.

◇ A good place to start is getting a referral from someone you know. Lacking such a personal connection, you can get names through doctors, hospitals, clinics, or graduate schools. Finally, there are the Yellow Pages or other forms of advertisement.

◇ If money is a problem, there are sliding-fee schedules. You can find therapists-in-training who will work with you at reduced rates. As you gather names, determine if the therapist's specialty meets your needs.

◇ Ask yourself if you prefer to work with a woman or a man. If you have an immediate feeling/response to that question, trust it. If not, gender probably doesn't matter to you.

◇ Make some appointments and shop around. Better to invest in an initial session with several therapists than to risk wasting a lot of time because of a hasty decision.

You can't choose the "right" therapist strictly by credentials or factual information. Here's where your intuition plays a part. During the first sessions, ask yourself: How do I *feel* with this person? . . . Is this someone I can talk to easily? . . . Do I feel heard? understood? . . . Are there any danger signals? The personal qualities of a therapist—presence, integrity, compassion, warmth, and openness—are as important as technical or theoretical expertise.

Once you've made a choice, remember it's not irrevocable. Time will reveal more. As your relationship develops, you'll learn the scope of your therapist's capacities and the depth of his or her emotional support.

In *Thou Shalt Not Be Aware*, author Alice Miller writes, "The ability [of a therapist] to perceive and understand someone else's suffering depends more than anything else on the degree to which he/she has experienced the suffering of his/her own childhood."

Above all, trust yourself. If at any point you feel dissatisfied, upset, or misunderstood by your therapist, say so. If he or she doesn't listen to you, doesn't acknowledge your feelings, or remains defensive, you're probably with the wrong person.

The "expert" is not always right. The old view of the professional as all-powerful and all-knowing has contributed to many people's fear of getting help. True, the client is vulnerable, and a therapist's competence is essential, but the therapist is also human. You are the ultimate authority. If something feels wrong and you can't work it out, leave. You'll find help elsewhere.

Taking those first steps is tough, no matter who you are. But waiting won't make it any easier.

I remember how tentative my first approach to getting help was. I enrolled in a class to learn about a type of therapy I was interested in but too afraid to pursue directly. What was I afraid of? The unknown. And I was ashamed to reveal my problems to another human being. I kidded myself into believing I could get what I needed through generalized information. I was still hiding. But fortunately, events did not unfold the way I planned. At the first class meeting, it was apparent that enrollment was insufficient. So the class was canceled.

As the students dispersed, I panicked. My fragile link to therapy was vanishing! With only seconds remaining, I sacrificed my self-protection and courageously approached the teacher, asking, "Would you happen to know of a therapist in this area I could work with?" What bravery! I could hardly believe those words were coming out of my mouth.

She said, "Yes," and that was the beginning. Those circumstances worked together to further my growth. I'm convinced now that on that day as well as many others before and since, I was assisted by a Power greater than myself to move forward.

> Until one is committed there is hesitancy, the chance to draw back, always ineffectiveness. Concerning all acts of initiative (and creation) there is one elementary truth the ignorance of which kills countless ideas and splendid plans: that the moment one definitely commits oneself, Providence moves too. All sorts of things then occur to help one that would never otherwise have occurred. A whole stream of events issue from the decision, raising in one's favor all manner of unforeseen incidents and meetings and material assistance which no one could have dreamed would come his way. WHATEVER YOU CAN DO OR DREAM YOU CAN, BEGIN IT. BOLDNESS HAS GENIUS, POWER AND MAGIC IN IT. BEGIN IT NOW."
>
> —Goethe

CHAPTER 2

PAIN'S PURPOSE

Making the decision to begin therapy is deciding to face what hurts, what's causing pain. Since we're accustomed to viewing pain as our enemy, some people entering therapy may feel like brave soldiers going into battle, while others may feel meek and small, approaching an unknown adversary.

Pain itself, emotional or physical, is something we fear, hate, resent, and try to avoid—with all our being. We fear suffering because it hurts, and because we don't see its purpose. It strikes us as cruel, insulting, overwhelming—often making us feel helpless. We perceive pain as something that shouldn't be, something gone wrong and needing to be fixed right away. That belief actually increases our suffering by making us struggle against pain, thinking we should be able to stop it. When we can't, feelings of shame and self-pity add to our distress.

Our culture teaches us to avoid pain, and to *think* of it as avoidable. Too often our families reinforce that belief, causing conflict and confusion. Many men never get into therapy, because it would mean admitting they feel pain and then showing it. Very young they were taught the old adage "Boys don't cry." Sometimes girls get the same message.

In therapy sessions, every time my client Doug began to feel pain or the need to cry, he was overwhelmed with shame and the feeling of doing something wrong. I watched as his body tensed, his breathing faltered, and he fixed his gaze. The hint of tears, which had barely begun to form, disappeared in a flash, as if he had ordered them to go away.

Doug said, "My father forced me to be tough, like he was. Whenever I felt sad about anything and started to cry, he'd yell, 'Shut up!' It was so hard to stop crying . . . sometimes I couldn't, but I had to try. I was afraid he'd hit me."

Doug learned that crying was shameful and dangerous. Feeling sad was dangerous, because it led to crying. Pretty soon he shut down emotionally whenever he began to feel pain. My acceptance of Doug's tears, and encouragement of their expression, was completely foreign to him. It took time for him to get used to the support, and to trust it.

It's hard to accept a positive side to pain. But what if it does have a purpose? What if it's more than the senseless attack upon us we perceive it to be?

Pleasure may be what we search for, but pain is what we learn from. Good times make us feel joyous, free, or satisfied with life, but they rarely change who we are. Bad times, often the catalysts for transformation, create pressure to achieve something new, or to get out of a situation, or to redefine an aspect of ourselves.

Pain is our protector and teacher. Its purpose is to let us know something needs attention. Just as physical pain signals a threat to our bodies, emotional pain is also a signal, but its message isn't always easy to grasp. Lacking understanding and acceptance, most people are afraid and ashamed. Their minds are not open to learning, so pain's lessons are missed.

Pain pushes us from the inside out. Sometimes it nudges us gently; other times it shoves brutally. Either way it makes us move, often to run away.

"This tendency to avoid problems, and the emotional suffering inherent in them, is the primary basis of all human mental illness," says Scott Peck in *The Road Less Traveled*. But, he goes on to say, "It is only because of problems that we grow mentally and spiritually. It is through the pain of confronting and resolving problems that we learn."

When our methods of running away stop working, and pain persists, we eventually ask ourselves, What is going on here? Why is this happening? What can I do to change it?

We say we accept change as a part of life, but we really don't—because it's often so painful. Change means letting go of something familiar, to reach for something unknown. It requires a loss of some kind. The loss may be tangible like a job, a home, a relationship with another person, or it may be something less tangible—a way of being, a part of our "self," our identity, our self-image.

For example, if you're a person for whom being safe and secure is of great value, but you want to have new, adventurous experiences, you'll have to take risks. In order to take risks, you'll need to let go of your attachment to feeling safe and secure. This is not easy. It will probably feel frightening. The extent to which we are attached to something determines how much it hurts to let it go. In order to change, to grow, you will have to let go of the familiar, face the unknown, and feel some pain.

I remember sometimes as a child my whole body ached, and I didn't know why. My father would say, "Don't worry, it's just growing pains." That reassuring idea comforted me. I then understood there was a reason for my pain—I was growing. I felt proud to know I was growing, and that I was big enough to suffer a little for it. And I was in awe that my growing was taking place beyond my control—I was part of something bigger than myself.

Emotional growth takes place in the same way. Sometimes, as adults, we must suffer emotional growing pains, whether we want to or not, whether we fight them or embrace them. Once we realize that pain can bring us something positive, it's easier to stop fearing and fighting it. When we stop seeing pain as our enemy, we cease to be its victims, and it actually becomes less painful.

Suffering signals a problem whose source may be a current situation, or something from the past, or both. It's up to us to decipher the message pain is attempting to communicate. The therapist's role is to help us in the decoding process.

One of my clients, Jack, complained of daily headaches at work, and of feeling angry much of the time. He could have looked no further than the headaches, taken lots of aspirin, and continued to snap at his co-workers. Instead we began to look further, and found he was resentful because he felt taken advantage of and unappreciated. His boss was a cold, rough, aggressive man who only pointed out Jack's mistakes, never praising his accomplishments. That hurt Jack, and made him angry.

Jack was in pain. Obvious solutions to the problem were: (1) talk to the boss and (2) if there was no change, leave the job. Easy? Maybe. Maybe not.

Jack could neither bring himself to speak to the boss nor to leave his job. He said, "Why bother talking? The boss won't listen to me. He'll just criticize me for complaining. Even if he did listen, it wouldn't change anything. That's just the way it is."

"In that case," I asked, "why not leave?"

Jack answered, "Oh, my last boss was worse than he is, and another one probably wouldn't be any better. That's just how bosses are."

Jack was stuck in his pain, anger, and headaches, with no apparent way out. We decided to work on the only solution left—his reactions to the boss's behavior.

As we began to explore Jack's feelings and life story, it came out that in Jack's childhood his father was much like his boss—critical, mean, abusive—rarely giving him a kind word and often being cutting or derisive. As a child, Jack was literally stuck in his situation. If he tried to protest, his father became more oppressive, sometimes violent.

As an adult Jack continued to react the same way in the presence of abusive authority figures. He still felt "stuck" because he'd never resolved that trauma.

When Jack talked for the first time about his relationship with his father, he released tears and rage that he had held inside for years. We saw that the pain he experienced on the job was signaling two problems, one in his current work environment, and the other in past feelings and experiences yet unresolved.

How does one resolve the past if the events themselves can no longer be changed? In therapy, the process is called "working through," bringing a trauma to consciousness. Working through is a multi-level experience of remembering, feeling, understanding, expressing, and finally allowing someone else to acknowledge and share feelings. The process in itself heals. Furthermore, revealing past traumas clarifies current predicaments.

In Jack's case, for example, once he worked through his relationship with his father, he no longer felt powerless in the presence of his boss. His overreacting lessened, and he understood where the intensity of his reactions had come from. He could let go of the generalization he had about "authorities," and was able to see his boss and their relationship more clearly.

Jack's decision then was to confront his boss and express dissatisfaction with the verbal abuse and lack of positive acknowledgment. The boss was unreceptive to Jack's approach, defending himself and putting Jack down for "making a big thing out of nothing."

Of course, Jack was hurt and disappointed by this reaction, but not crushed as he previously might have been. Instead of using the incident to confirm his old, negative belief about "all bosses," Jack concluded that *this* boss was very unpleasant to work for.

We continued to work on Jack's sense of self-worth and personal power. Eventually he chose to leave the job, believing that he could find a more supportive and caring work environment. And he did.

It's not necessary to know why you are unhappy or in pain, in order to seek help. Jack's case is a good example. All he knew was that he had headaches and was angry all the time at work. That was the starting point. Even if he had known the current source of his anger (the boss), chances are he wouldn't have, alone, discovered the origin of his larger problem. If he did make the connection between his father and his boss, the suppressed feelings would still have been inaccessible to him without help.

Present-day situations often act as catalysts, stirring up feelings from the past, especially so because we unconsciously seek out and create circumstances which, in some way, parallel those of the past. This explains why people keep finding themselves faced over and over with the same issues in different relationships or different jobs, and why we have recurring dreams.

I know that seems uncanny, and it is mysterious—the mystery of the unconscious. We unconsciously try to bring to light what was forgotten so it can be healed. Pain is pointing the way. *But until we recognize a particular pattern, no resolution is possible.* We are doomed to continue the reenactment process, suffering the same pain over and over, never knowing why, nor believing it can be any better.

Whenever an emotional reaction is "bigger," longer-lasting or more overwhelming than is appropriate for the situation, we may assume that pain from the past has been triggered.

Past pain can also manifest itself in many other ways:

◊ A black cloud of feelings hanging over your daily life: depression, anxiety, emptiness, boredom, apathy, despair, dissatisfaction, frustration, resentment, or self-pity

- ◇ Frequent, dramatic ups-and-downs of your emotions and behavior, resulting in a chaotic lifestyle
- ◇ Mysterious, irrational overreacting to events, situations, or personalities
- ◇ Recurring patterns of conflict in painful or unfulfilling love relationships
- ◇ Compulsive behavior and addictions to alcohol, drugs, food, cigarettes, work, sex, relationships, money, and so on
- ◇ Unreasonable and intense fears, panics, and nightmares
- ◇ Isolated lifestyle—difficulty or disinterest in making, or sustaining, friendships or sexual love relationships
- ◇ Chronic underachievement, underemployment—an ongoing sense of failure
- ◇ Criminal behavior, in some instances
- ◇ A physical illness with no clear-cut cause
- ◇ Some forms of sexual dysfunction
- ◇ Inability to recover after loss
- ◇ Inability to spend time alone

You probably recognize pain-detectors in your life. If so, you're already on your way by admitting the truth to yourself. Many people live with pain and problems in the background all their lives. Some accept this as normal, and without question. Some are dimly aware of what's wrong, but are resigned to their lot in life. Others are too ashamed to admit their pain to anyone, too afraid to seek help, or feel it will be too expensive. Still others don't believe that help is available at any price. But help *is* available. With compassionate and skillful guidance, even pain that has been lifelong can be healed.

It may be hard to believe that the past can still be affecting you, but it is. Most chronic problems in adulthood are those that have grown slowly over time, out of their beginnings in childhood. Those beginnings are probably unclear to you now, especially if your memory is sketchy, or you don't think there was any trauma in your childhood.

Trauma is anything causing deep shock, pain, or overwhelming upset on one or more levels: physical, mental, emotional, spiritual. But trauma takes many forms: sometimes it is obvious, at other times covert. It can occur only once, or frequently. Sometimes trauma can be so subtle and pervasive that it's simply part of "the way things were." A skillful therapist can help you to link the past with the present. As a child you didn't have words to express the traumas you went through; as an adult you can find those words.

Recently, the media have raised our awareness of two of the most devastating forms of trauma suffered by children—physical abuse and sexual abuse. Despite this heightened consciousness, however, many people who were abused children continue to deny that they were. Maybe you are one of them. Why is this denial so common? I think there are three main reasons:

1. Most people don't realize that what they endured, and considered normal, was in fact abusive. Neglect, for example, is a form of passive abuse, often unrecognized. Also, many forms of punishment are abusive, but since they are common practice and carried out in the name of discipline, they are accepted by the child and buried in his or her memory as deserved punishment. An abused child merely bears whatever happens, justifying and rationalizing it by taking on the guilt for it.

   "I deserved it," one client told me. "Dad only hit me when I did something wrong. I always knew when I'd be getting that strap."

   Another client said, "Mom was under a lot of pressure with us kids. I knew she loved us, but sometimes she just couldn't handle us. That's when she'd fly into a rage, and the hitting would start."

2. People compare themselves to news reports on television, and conclude, "I didn't have it that bad; others had it worse." Yes, there are always worse cases, but abuse doesn't have to be dramatic to be harmful.
3. Accepting the reality of having been abused is shocking. The concept of abuse carries a terrible stigma—people don't want to admit to it, to themselves or to anyone else.

It's true that children need limits and order. And of course, sometimes they will break rules and create chaos. But nothing justifies prolonged, violent beatings, the use of objects for hitting, or the humiliation of slaps in the face. Those actions indicate a parent who is out of control emotionally, venting rage by wielding power over a helpless child. A parent who behaves in these ways is acting out his or her unresolved problems, and the child pays the price.

Abused children feel hurt, terrified, betrayed, abandoned, and humiliated. Long-term effects shouldn't be underestimated. Adults who were abused in childhood suffer from a core feeling of worthlessness and shame that, in a vicious cycle, feeds the need to deny the truth of the past.

If you were abused, you may see problems in your life but, unaware of their source, wonder why you can't solve them. You may struggle with nightmares, panic attacks, alcoholism, or other addictions. Intimate relationships may be especially difficult. You may feel trapped in a pattern of verbally or physically abusive relationships. Sustaining intimacy can seem impossible; trusting and being vulnerable might feel dangerous. You may withdraw to an emotional distance in order to feel safe, or you may eventually withdraw from relationships altogether.

The trauma of sexual abuse in childhood further complicates adult interpersonal relationships. This form of abuse is often denied by "forgetting" or minimizing, particularly because it is not always obvious. I helped one woman who said things like this about an uncle: "Oh, he never *really* did anything to me—sexually, I mean. Actually I can't remember very well, except that he always looked at me strangely, and liked to be alone with me a lot. When he touched me, I felt uncomfortable."

Sexual violation can take place subtly, in a hands-off manner, through verbal innuendo, eye contact, or gesture. A parent who is emotionally overinvested in his or her child, due to death of the spouse or to unresolved marital conflict, is unknowingly being abusive to the child, both emotionally and sexually. This child becomes a surrogate spouse, forced to fulfill the parent's unmet needs as he or she is brought into the adult world prematurely.

Sexuality is such a personal and sensitive subject that most people have difficulty talking about it at all. But talking about it is the only way to bring out hidden abuse so it can be healed.

You may have been the victim of sexual abuse if you experience: sexual dysfunctions; excessive fear, panic, or revulsion associated with sex; numbness or a sudden shutdown of sexual feelings; flashbacks; sexual promiscuity, compulsivity, prostitution; excessive awareness and attention to sexuality in general; inattention to, or withdrawal from, sexuality in general.

Denying and avoiding the truth enables people to hide from feelings of pain and shame. It also helps protect the image of a happy childhood, which we all would like to maintain. But *facing* the truth opens the door for change. It allows the past to be worked through so that hiding and running are no longer necessary, and today's problems can be solved. Every trauma is devastating in its own way, and if not dealt with has far-reaching effects.

Childhood for Julie was a confusing time. When she was six, her parents divorced, and from then on she lived with her mother. According to Julie, there always seemed to be men around the house. She was never comfortable with her mother's boyfriends, but the worst one was Drew. In her words, "He always liked to take me out for drives and buy me presents. The gifts were okay, but the drives were the awful part. He'd talk to me in a strange voice, and do things to me, and tell me to do things to him. Back at home, I'd catch him looking at me. It was scary, and it made me sick."

The story of Drew only came back to Julie at age thirty-four, after two years of therapy. The feelings that followed were intense and painful—terror, confusion, humiliation, rage, acute sadness, and loneliness.

Before therapy Julie led a wild life, including a lot of sexual partners. "It seemed fine in my twenties," she said wistfully. "I never had a boyfriend for longer than a few months, but I didn't care. I worked in a nightclub as a waitress—there were always plenty of new guys around! I didn't really respect any of them. I just used them. It actually made me feel powerful, in a way.

"Then I met Robert, and a weird thing happened. After the usual few months, I didn't want to end the relationship and neither did he! That in itself was a miracle. Then suddenly I stopped wanting to make love. I felt so confused and ashamed about it. I didn't know what to do at first, so I just didn't tell Robert, and forced myself to have sex with him anyway. It was awful. I didn't feel anything except fear—I was absolutely frozen. I tried fantasizing but the only images that appeared were violent ones, and that upset me more. It got worse and worse. Pretty soon it made me sick to have him even touch me. That's when I decided to get help."

In therapy, Julie's defensive freeze started to thaw. She was able to tell Robert what was happening, and fortunately he was willing to work on it with her. They came in together for a few sessions. Robert needed support and information himself, so that he could understand Julie and be patient through her recovery process.

"Talking about my feelings to him was so embarrassing," she said. "I almost left him, to get away from the shame. He wanted to leave too, and I don't blame him. Luckily, so far neither of us has. Actually, because of my therapy, Robert has become much more open about his own problems, and that's been good.

"I realize now that what was going on in my relationship with Robert had happened with all my past boyfriends. We'd start to get close, and I'd shut down sexually. I never knew then that it was a pattern. I just thought I'd gotten turned off because I was bored, so I went on to the next guy. Really, I was terrified."

The trauma of sexual abuse in Julie's past had been running, and ruining, her life. She was unable to be emotionally and sexually intimate with anyone until she uncovered the protective defenses she'd formed in childhood. Then she had to work through the long-buried feelings associated with the sexual violations.

All childhood traumas need to be dealt with sensitively. Although there are commonalities, circumstances combine differently to form each individual's story.

Another trauma that has lifelong consequences is the death of a parent. Even though death is acknowledged as a tragedy, its emotional impact is rarely processed at the time, and its ramifications go unrecognized. To us, as adults, death is incomprehensible. It is even less comprehensible to children. A sudden death is shocking and disorienting; there is no opportunity to prepare for the loss. A slow death forces the child to witness the parent's suffering and deterioration, and may also bring terrifying cycles of separation, during hospitalizations.

If you experienced the loss of a parent, you may have "forgotten" the whole time period surrounding the death. This form of forgetting is an unconscious protection against the pain of the memories. Or you may have sudden rushes of memory and feelings, brought on by a "triggering" event. If those feelings are not processed, they simply resubmerge into the unconscious.

A young child whose parent dies distorts the facts through lack of understanding. He or she may feel guilty, taking responsibility for the death. A child who is secretly glad the parent is gone may feel tremendous shame. Children feel unloved and deserted when a parent dies, as if the parent would not have "left" if she or he had really loved the child. There is also a deep, hidden rage, especially in the case of suicide and in deaths related to alcoholism and drug addiction, where the decision to die is, or appears to be, in the parent's own hands.

Scars from loss of a parent take many forms later on. Among them are chronic insecurity, extreme fear of abandonment, lack of self-confidence, excessive guilt, codependency, and addictions.

Therapy provides an opportunity to unravel the twists and knots of memory, bring out forgotten details, look closely at what took place in the past, and discover its effects.

"But," you may be saying, "I don't know if I *want* to dig up all that pain. Why should I? It's just too much. It's not worth it. I went through it once—that's enough!"

Everyone feels that way at times, and most people do try hard to leave the past behind. Unfortunately, it follows us wherever we go, revealing itself in all the symptoms mentioned. The reason you're reading this book is that leaving your past buried has left your emotional problems unsolved. The past is a part of you. All of it—even the pain—is you.

To the extent that you are cut off from your past, you are cutting off some of your energy, your depth, your possibilities for love, success, and fulfillment in every way. Sure, you can choose to not discover your past, but the only way to change conditions with roots in the past is to acknowledge those roots, cultivate and work with them, so you can continue to grow unrestrained. Of course, it takes courage and commitment to change, but the results are worth the effort.

Begin by looking at your memories. The acute traumas of physical abuse and death, just described, are responsible for only a portion of the emotional problems burdening adults. Other influences, however, though sometimes less obvious, can be harmful when endured throughout a young life. They are too numerous to explain in detail, but a few are:

- ◊ Major illnesses or accidents involving parents, children, or siblings
- ◊ Passive (nonviolent) parental alcoholism or addiction
- ◊ Prolonged absence of one or both parents
- ◊ Verbal abuse, frequent criticism
- ◊ Constant arguing, conflict, or violence between the parents
- ◊ Rigid, parental overcontrol and discipline
- ◊ Lack of parental control and setting of limits
- ◊ Inattention to, rejection or ridicule of a child's feelings and needs
- ◊ Threats in the form of words, hostile glances or gestures, harsh tones of voice

When negative behaviors or circumstances are ongoing, even though they don't stand out as dramatic events, they are harmful. Daily life, taken for granted as it is, is a powerful conditioning force. The child's whole environment becomes traumatic, and its damaging effects are cumulative.

Children don't have the resources that adults have for handling problems and dealing with stress. Children are able to *defend* themselves only by *suppressing* their confused, painful feelings, and by *adapting* to circumstances. But defensive behavior, necessary for survival, is extremely detrimental to growth.

As Alice Miller says, in *The Drama of the Gifted Child:*

> It is precisely because a child's feelings are so strong, that they cannot be repressed without serious consequences. The stronger a prisoner is, the thicker the prison walls have to be, which impede or completely prevent later emotional growth.

If you have ongoing emotional problems now, but few or no childhood memories, suppression has probably occurred. It is not uncommon to have little or no memory of childhood, or segments of childhood. In therapy, memories reappear. You may have thoughts or mental pictures of incidents, but no feelings about those incidents; the feelings have been blocked. But they are not lost. When you choose to explore the past in therapy, your feelings are retrieved.

As feelings and memories emerge, they may confuse you. In your family, your parents may have attempted to maintain a façade of happiness and control. Although many parents try to hide the truth of their conflicts from their children, the children sense trouble nonetheless.

Some families maintain an illusion of being "perfect." They are chaotic behind closed doors but perceived as "ideal" by everyone in the neighborhood. A pseudo-happy family is not a healthy one. Any form of secrecy is debilitating to children. As a child, *you* may have known or felt the truth of what was going on around you, but were unable to talk about it or make sense of it because everyone pretended that things were okay. Conflict is a normal part of human relationships. Anger and its expression and resolution should be modeled by parents, in order for children to know that *their* anger is acceptable. *They need to learn how to express anger appropriately, and understand that relationships survive, even grow, through conflict.*

Earl and Betty had been together for two years. At our first meeting they sat very close together, touching a lot, laughing and joking. To most people they looked happy, and, as a matter of fact, they were fairly happy much of the time. They had a solid friendship, common interests, and a good sexual relationship.

So why were they coming to see me? When they tried to articulate the problem, both became uncomfortable. Earl averted his eyes, looking trapped and desperate, as if he wanted to disappear behind the sofa or out the door. Betty fidgeted and smiled anxiously, glancing at Earl, leaning toward him as he seemed to pull farther and farther away.

Betty began: "We go in cycles where everything will be fine and then suddenly, he'll change. He walks around with a scowl on his face, and he won't touch me. When he talks, he snaps in a mean, sarcastic voice. I get so hurt and upset. It's confusing, too. I start trying to figure out what happened, and if I did something wrong. When I ask him, 'What's wrong?' he says, 'Nothing.' Then I go nuts inside, and don't know what to do."

Earl breaks in, "Yeah, and then instead of dropping the subject, she keeps pushing. She questions me in this nagging voice, accusing me of things. She acts insecure and clinging and mad, all at the same time. I don't know what to say, and I wish she'd just leave me alone. She stirs stuff up, and it makes everything worse. Then I start thinking, 'Maybe we should break up.' "

Betty goes on, "And then he *says* maybe we should break up, and that's the last straw."

"What happens next?" I ask, barely able to get in a word.

"Sometimes we just have a cold war, for hours or days," Betty answers. "And I hate that. It's lonely and awful. We're both mad and ignore each other or throw dagger looks."

Says Earl, "When we get to bed at night, we usually have sex. Sex always makes us feel good. [They smile at each other.] It sort of puts a Band-Aid on the problem. By morning, we're less angry, and eventually the problem fades away."

Betty implores, "But these bad times seem to be happening more often and lasting longer."

In a softer voice, Earl adds, "Once in a while, when she questions me about what's wrong, I'll figure it out, and tell her. Then afterwards, I'm glad I did, and we get along better. Actually, we get along well a lot of the time. I don't want you to think we have a bad relationship or something."

Earl's last comment was a bit of "impression management." It was important to him to be seen as successful in his relationship, and "success" to him meant absence of conflict.

As we worked together, we discovered that, like many couples, Earl and Betty could not get angry at each other directly. In childhood, each had learned the same lesson: "Anger is bad."

Their families had taught them that in different ways.

Said Earl, "In my house, no one ever got angry. My mother's attitude was to be nice to everybody. It seemed right, but then she had nervous breakdowns, so I guess it wasn't. My father was really domineering and forceful, but I never saw him get angry. He'd just withdraw."

Betty's story was the opposite: "My father and mother yelled at each other all the time. I hated hearing them fight. It felt like the world was coming to an end. My father yelled the loudest, and my mother would yell at him to be quiet, because of the neighbors. He also yelled at me and my brother and sister, but we were never allowed to say anything back. I was really scared of my father."

Betty and Earl were afraid of anger—their own and each other's. To Earl, open conflict was foreign, and signified the end of the relationship. For Betty, it was not only terrifying, but also shameful and forbidden. Their fears were responsible for the impasse they had reached. They suppressed the intensity of their feelings, yet communicated them *indirectly*—through withdrawal, body language, tones of voice, and other manipulative ploys. Sometimes they were able to "fix" the situation temporarily through sex, but in the long run, they needed help.

It took time to work through their fear and shame, which had become associated with anger and had blocked its expression. They both needed reassurance from the other that the relationship was not threatened, that neither one was leaving, and that they still loved each other.

I gave them the language to communicate more directly—ways to further resolve conflict instead of stalemating it. For example, addressing Earl, I said: "When Betty asks you, 'What's wrong?' I know you feel threatened, and you defend yourself by saying, 'Nothing's wrong.' Betty gets more upset because she knows that's not true, and she's frustrated because there's nothing she can say or do. You could try saying, 'I don't know what's wrong right now; I need some time to think about it.' Or, 'I'm afraid to tell you what's wrong, because you'll get mad, or it'll hurt your feelings.' "

And to Betty, I said, "Instead of pushing Earl for answers, or trying to second-guess him, it would help if you told him how *you* feel. You might say, 'I'm scared, because I sense something's wrong, and I don't know what it is. I'm afraid you're mad at me for something I did.' "

With practice, they both learned to express their feelings more openly, and to tolerate the other's reaction even when it was an angry one.

Betty commented on the change: "It actually feels good to get angry now. It's much better to let it out than it was to keep it in. It's still scary when Earl raises his voice with me, but at least now I know what he's thinking, and we don't disconnect."

Earl added, "The best part for me is that we can have disagreements and they *end*, but the relationship goes on, and it's not damaged like I thought it would be. We keep talking until the conflict is resolved, and it's all over much faster than before. In my family, *nothing* ever ended, it just got buried, and the resentments grew. This is definitely an improvement."

Finding the way to healthy communication of anger is a goal of most people in therapy. This is because most people come from families in which anger was suppressed, expressed indirectly, or expressed abusively.

There are families that allow anger but censor other feelings. In some, sadness and crying are suppressed; in others, fear is not "permitted." Often, expressions of exuberant joy or natural sexuality are met with disapproval. Whenever anything is unacceptable, it is suppressed or acted out in some way. The confusion resulting from hypocrisy and double messages can be very damaging. Children know intuitively what is going on around them.

When parents deny the truth, children doubt themselves and they grow up to be adults who don't recognize or trust their own feelings. Ignorance on the part of parents is clearly the cause of much damage done to children. However, even the most loving and committed parents cannot create a perfect environment. Some suffering is inevitable for all of us. It is part of being human.

Michael Lerner puts it this way in his book *Surplus Powerlessness:*

> The child discovers itself in the eyes of its parents, but most parents do not really see the child. Many parents are simply not open to the beauty, excitement, curiosity, and wonder that they could experience with their children . . . most parents are refugees from the pain of their work experiences and the pain of their childhoods. They enter each encounter with their own children in a state of inner pain and frustration. Their attention is scattered and their perceptions blunted by dramas that have been going on in their lives long before their children entered the scene.

You may feel like defending your parents at this point. You don't have to. We are examining the past for the purpose of healing, not indictment. All families provide both positives and negatives—sometimes more of one than the other. Your parents may have been very caring. You might have had a lot of wonderful experiences and happy times as a child. Elucidating the problem areas does not invalidate the love you received. Given their emotional resources and social influences, parents do the best they can. No one is perfect. Much of what they offered is a result of the parenting they received. Furthermore, childhood traumas can also take place outside the family. You have the right to rediscover the events of your life.

When remembering your own personal history, don't compare it to the circumstances of others. It is impossible to evaluate or measure the suffering of one person against that of another. What counts is your life and your feelings. Comparison invalidates unique, individual experience. What you felt as traumatic was traumatic, regardless of what others went through. Whether or not there was any overt abuse in your history, at the very least you were subjected to a process of conditioning—an inevitable part of being in a family and in a culture. Everyone's development is influenced by surroundings, by verbal and nonverbal messages to "be this way," or, "don't be that way." While some behaviors are praised and encouraged, others are ignored, discouraged, or actually punished.

Those messages and surroundings, to varying degrees, either nourish and support the innate personality, or oppose and thwart it. A nourishing environment fosters love, security, creativity, healthy relationships, and freedom of expression. Natural talents and abilities are discovered, guided, and given room to grow.

In a less healthy environment, conditioning goes contrary to the child's true nature. Squelched and controlled, the natural self is comparable to a tree that has been bound and pruned to conform to a particular shape. Its growth is distorted and stunted, its freedom and spontaneity have been taken away. What would have been its natural shape is never known. Much potential for richness in adult life can be lost this way—sometimes permanently. Lost potential means creativity never discovered, abilities never developed, careers never lived. It means stunted emotional growth in the world of relationships. Finally, and perhaps most subtly, it means the loss of naturalness, spontaneity, and confidence, which provide easy access to feelings, and the ability to express them openly and fearlessly.

Without access to the deeper parts of ourselves, we are limiting our lives, unaware of any alternatives. We deny some parts of our beings, while exaggerating others. We attempt to live up to people's expectations, or to follow an idea or social stereotype of who we "should" be. We never know why we're dissatisfied, depressed, or resentful. We feel empty and unauthentic, like something is missing; and something *is* missing.

What would a person be like who comes from a truly healthy upbringing? Let's look at a hypothetical example, and call her "Raina." Raina is a 54-year-old pianist. She lives with her husband, Darryl, in a small town in northern California. They have three children—all adults, now living away from home. Darryl and Raina moved from San Francisco after their youngest child left home.

Raina remembers her childhood: "Our house was the place where other kids in the neighborhood gathered. We had a warm living room with a fireplace, and there always seemed to be people around. My father was a teacher and my mother an artist. They valued love, creativity, and individuality. We had a comfortable life, but the emphasis was not on financial or material success, it was more on doing what felt right.

"They both loved music, and when I was young, they noticed I liked music, too, so they bought child-size instruments for me to play. I really only like the piano, and they didn't force me into anything else. I wasn't crazy about practicing though, but they made me do it. I would get mad, but now I'm glad I learned the discipline. Creativity has been a source of strength and joy in my life.

"I tried to offer that same joy to my children, but not by force. I never wanted to make them live out my choices; they were allowed to make their own. Otherwise, they would be like obedient little robots. My parents were good models, but they always encouraged me to find my *own* way, at the same time being realistic and practical. They helped me discover what my real interests and talents were, and supported me in developing them. When I rebelled, they didn't try to stifle me or reject me—I always knew they were there.

"I'm not saying that everything was smooth sailing at home. We had plenty of fights, all of us. But what I liked was that we were never allowed to be abusive to each other. My parents told us how they felt and what they thought, and taught us to do the same. It felt safe to be there. I knew they loved me, and I knew they loved each other. I'm sure that's why I've had such a good marriage. Darryl and I don't hold back very much. We believe in saying what we feel, both positive and negative. We try to support each other, but also give each other space."

Unfortunately, in our society, people like Raina, who enjoyed the benefits of a nourishing childhood, are the exception, not the rule. It's also important to realize, however, that no one has an ideal, problem-free childhood, just as no one has a problem-free adulthood. When unraveling the past in therapy, and feeling its pain, it's natural to think, "If only my parents had been this way or that way, everything could have been perfect." Everything could have been *different* and maybe better, but not perfect. A child is a small person, born into a big world, of which he or she has almost no control and little understanding. Yet children are called upon to rise to the occasion and adjust to circumstances. No small task!

The specifics of our circumstances, and the ways we deal with them, form our better, as well as our lesser, qualities. The expression "Suffering builds character" is not always comforting, but is often true. There *is* a positive side to pain, if we grow through it.

For example, a person who has suffered tremendously in childhood may become a sensitive and compassionate adult. Or, a child from a hostile home environment who finds refuge in getting a job or learning an art may grow up to be a very successful professional. Many people develop a good sense of humor as a by-product of the attempt to mitigate distress.

To nurture yourself or your children means to accept life in its totality, without denying that life has joy and pain. The concept of living pain-free is just a fantasy, so a more realistic ideal to pursue might be to reach the point where you can experience life on its terms—whatever life gives each day—and work with it.

Some people come to therapy cherishing the illusion that their childhood was happy, when actually it wasn't. Their parents tried to cope with hardship and shielded their children by smiling and *acting* happy all the time. Children in these families receive implicit instructions to act happy even if they don't feel happy. They learn to pretend—the same way the adults are pretending. The children are abandoned emotionally, because a whole range of feelings are being overlooked. Children feel shame and confusion about "negative" feelings, hide them, and are left alone with an emotional burden deep inside. The problem becomes evident only later when emotions, inaccessible directly, reveal themselves in countless other ways.

Dr. Gerald May, in his book *Addiction and Grace*, says:

> The implications of accepting pain are significant, in dealing with specific addictions, but they become massive in terms of our basic attitude toward life. In our society, we have come to believe that discomfort always means something is wrong. We are conditioned to believe that feelings of distress, pain, deprivation, yearning, and longing mean something is wrong with the way we are living our lives. Conversely, we are convinced that a rightly lived life must give us serenity, completion, and fulfillment. Comfort means "right" and distress means "wrong." The influence of such convictions is stifling to the human spirit. Individually and collectively, we must somehow recover the truth. The truth is, we were never meant to be completely satisfied.

Though neither childhood nor adulthood can be perfect, they *can* be better. Fortunately, our awareness of children's needs is increasing, so parenting, at least for some, is improving. And, even though we as adults can't relive our pasts, many of us are reclaiming our deeper, real selves through the psychological and spiritual healing processes.

To be cut off from any part of oneself, including the past, creates a rift in the psyche, which eventually becomes intolerable. Stress symptoms begin to show. Through symptoms, pain points to a problem that needs healing. Symptoms are potential windows to the self within—to the soul in pain. The human spirit, even when it's been suppressed and stunted, cannot be totally denied. Like blades of grass pushing their way through cracks in concrete, nature prevails even under the least hospitable conditions.

What appears on the surface to be an isolated weed of a problem is not isolated at all. Instead, it's a messenger from underground, communicating the existence of a subterranean world.

In order to live a full, healthy, successful life, we must have access to our "whole, real self." We must break open the concrete to allow the plant to flourish. Being "whole" means having the freedom and scope we were born to have—feeling deeply connected to self, to others, and to the spiritual dimension of life. Being "real" means being humbly aware of the profound experience we are part of. It means having the capacity to express the full spectrum of feelings, honestly and appropriately.

As Alice Miller writes in *The Drama of the Gifted Child*, "The true opposite of depression is not gaiety or absence of pain, but vitality—the freedom to experience spontaneous feelings. . . . But this freedom cannot be achieved if the childhood roots are cut off."

It's not necessary to live passively, resigned to frustration and unhappiness. By opening the doors to the deeper self, old wounds can be healed and inner resources for change, creativity, and joy can be set free.

In the healing process of psychotherapy, we unburden ourselves of leftover pain by working through it. Self-image, actions, and reactions are transformed miraculously. We free ourselves of destructive patterns and begin to nurture our hidden potential. The idea that nothing can be done about the effects of our past is simply a belief, not a fact. And it is an erroneous belief, based on fear and a lack of awareness of alternatives. But in order to find our way into our deepest selves and out of our limited lives, we must be willing to take some risks and feel some pain.

Alan Jones, in *Soulmaking*, writes, "A capacity for wonder and a readiness for pain are essential for the life of the soul."

Some people believe that pain is one of God's instruments to turn us in a spiritual direction. Despair and suffering have a way of forcing even the most cynical among us to call out for God.

At the very least, pain has a way of stripping us of our superficial preoccupations. Whether we choose to see suffering as an adversary to run from or a guide to grow from is up to us. Accepting pain as our teacher, we can follow its lead out of our resignation, resentment, and self-pity, into richer, deeper, and more satisfying lives.

CHAPTER 3

THE NEXT STEP: FEARS AND FEELINGS

A few years ago, I participated in an intense series of workshops for my own growth. When I enrolled, weeks prior to the start of the series, I was told the workshop had begun for me the moment I enrolled. That was a confusing concept at the time, but now I see how the same concept holds true in therapy: The very act of choosing to begin something (like therapy) sets the process of change in motion. It's as if the unconscious has waited patiently, and when finally given the go-ahead, it eagerly becomes conscious.

In the early stages of therapy, you unlock the door to your inner world. As that door opens, even just a crack, a narrow shaft of light falls into the darkness and illuminates a much larger area. You become aware in many new ways. Your mind prickles, stimulated by memories waking from their long sleep. You see fuzzy outlines of past events, hear muffled sounds. Your heart beats faster in anxious anticipation of this new experience—a mixture of excitement, fear, and longing for the answers you seek.

In this chapter, we'll see what it's like to find the missing link of the past.

Michael was accustomed to feeling only a narrow range of emotions; he never knew more, until he found cocaine. Suddenly he could get high and feel more intensity than he had ever before experienced. He quickly became addicted, and for many years, his life revolved around drugs and superficial sexual encounters with men he met in gay bars. Although he had intensity, he had no intimacy and no depth. After squandering himself in the vicious cycles of addiction, he finally bottomed out, got sober, and began therapy.

Michael's childhood had been a brutal one. His soul and body were trampled constantly by his violently abusive father. Michael's feelings—whenever he tentatively tried to make them known—were invalidated by criticism and ridicule. Other than that overall view, he had very little memory of the specifics of those days.

During one session, I asked if he wanted to try closing his eyes to help recall the past. He agreed. I spoke to him gently, while his eyes were closed, helping him to go back in time, remembering himself in his twenties, teens, and then even younger. I said, "As we grow up, we learn language, and skills, and take on responsibilities. We form values, and have a variety of experiences, but, as we grow up, we don't *lose* the child self, we just transform it. Something inside of us stays the same, some part of our self—the center, the soul or the mind—that feels and thinks and knows itself to be alive. Can you imagine that part of yourself, which has been there since long ago? Can you see that little boy?"

Michael's expression, even with his eyes closed, showed a deep sadness. The corners of his mouth and eyes turned downward, shadows seemed to darken his face. As he spoke, tears ran down his cheeks. "Yes," he said slowly, "I see myself. It's very dark and I'm all alone. It's so dark I can't see where I am. It's like a small room with no windows, or a cave, or a deep pit in the ground. I'm sitting down all hunched over with my knees pulled up—I can't move much. I can't see and I can't get out."

"How do you feel in there?" I asked.

He paused for a minute. "Cold," he answered.

"Anything else?"

He paused again, for a long time. "Very lonely. No one even knows I'm here. I'm just passing time. It's so sad."

Michael was naturally very upset after this session, but also thrilled by it. He made his first contact with the part of himself he had hidden so deep in his mind that he thought he'd lost it.

As we continued working together, he found more and more lost memories. One important one was that when his father became violent at home, Michael, terrified, would run and hide in the garage; it was his only defense. When battered by his father's ridicule, Michael's only choice was to be silent. Now, as he looked inside, he saw his frightened, little-boy self, silenced and locked up *within him*, just as, in the past, he had literally hidden in the dark garage for protection. Today, in the "cave" in his mind, he found the person he was before his growth was stunted. He rediscovered his capacity for feeling, a capacity blunted by years of abuse.

Many people describe themselves in images like Michael's—small, huddled in a dark pit or cave, lonely and unnoticed. It is an emotional moment of discovery. There's a great difference between remembering the past from an observer's perspective, and from a subjective view—remembering how you *felt* during those events. Most people are shocked at what they discover as they acknowledge the truth of what happened. There is also anger, shame, and fear—not only about what happened, but also about what didn't happen, and should have.

Sometimes the newly revealed self is mute; feelings arise but they can't be described. The words may be unavailable because they weren't learned at that time. Unless parents ask children how they feel, and teach them a vocabulary of responses, they simply have no language for feelings. Or a recollection can come from an age *before* language was learned. We are most vulnerable in our first few years of life; those important memories are usually experienced physically, as an ache or pain somewhere in the body, or through the senses—hunger, cold, darkness, emptiness, fatigue.

In Michael's case, he initially was aware of feeling cold and cramped—both physical sensations. We had several sessions before he was able to define emotions like sad and lonely.

Preverbal feelings require an inner process to translate them into adult, self-reflective vocabulary. The therapist assists in this process until understanding is achieved. People need to feel comforted when reexperiencing preverbal pain. What comforts them is not words, but love. Love is a vital part of therapy's healing. A truly compassionate therapist cares deeply about his or her clients, and a client recognizes this caring. Therapists demonstrate their love and compassion nonverbally—through eye contact, sitting close, and physical contact ranging from hand-holding to hugging. Physical contact is a delicate, but powerful, aspect of healing. The therapist determines the appropriate type of contact for each interaction, within each individual therapeutic relationship. Some therapists choose not to include touch at all in the parameters of their work. For those who do, contact can be very meaningful when it is done with respect and consideration for the client's greatest good.

Getting in touch with deeply buried feelings doesn't come easily, and some feelings show up quicker than others. Although Michael was able to feel loneliness and sadness when he remembered himself as a little boy hiding, he did not feel anger. I asked him, "How would you feel if you saw another little boy having to hide from his own father's violence?"

"Sad," he replied, "and angry. I'd want to scream at that father." It was easier for Michael to get in touch with anger through another person in his imagination. Many people can feel the pain of others more easily than their own. That's why some people cry only in movies, or when hearing sad stories. Their learned inhibition, which usually blocks feeling, grants permission because it is someone else's story.

For most people, the first connection to the self of their past, however painful, also brings great joy. It's like meeting a loved one after many years—a reunion of one part of the self with another. It's the recognition and realization of what was previously unconscious. This moment of reunion is very touching for me as a therapist and usually moves me to tears along with the person experiencing the reunion.

Michael realized that he, as an adult, had been oblivious to his feelings locked inside, just as his parents had been oblivious to him when he hid in the garage. The way we treat ourselves as adults reflects the way we were treated as children. Michael was ignored and abused, so he ignored his deeper feelings, accustomed to living with a part of himself cramped in the dark. He also habitually criticized himself, just as his father had done to him.

In subsequent sessions Michael came to realize: "My father not only scared and hurt me, but he also robbed me. I never experienced any soft feelings—love, affection, kindness—so I never looked for those feelings in my relationships with my lovers as an adult. 'Relationships!'—I've never even had relationships, I've just had sex! Now I'm beginning to get in touch with the part of me that is curious, playful, and enthusiastic. There was never time for that side of me. My parents were so busy dealing with their own chaotic lives, they didn't have the energy to take me places or play with me. I'm beginning to love my little-boy self. I want to do everything, feel everything. I want to really get to know people now, and eventually be with a man I can love, and who loves me. It's like I have a second chance. I'm excited about it!"

The joyful, creative self does develop when it finally has room to grow and breathe. That takes place only after the pain has been allowed to come in, and be expressed. In the first stages of therapy, when awareness of the inner self breaks through into consciousness, fears arise. This happens because in childhood certain thoughts and feelings were too intense, too dangerous—that's why they were suppressed. As the images emerge during this period, they seem as threatening as they were in the past. These fears are significant, and meaningful beyond their preliminary appearance. The *specific nature* of each fear is a clue to understanding the type of trauma about to be revealed. Here are some examples.

Loss of Control

Probably the most common fear, one that underlies many others, is loss of control. Internally, fear of losing control is experienced as dread—sometimes of a particular outcome, but more often of not being able to keep an appropriate lid on emotions.

A vague, but intense, terror of losing control is exemplified by Laura, a woman who had learned all her life to act in a "ladylike" manner. She was poised and articulate. Usually when her emotions surfaced, they were mild and short-lived. When she cried, she never sobbed, but instead cried silently, holding her breath in an attempt to push the pain away. The tears barely came out of her eyes before she fiercely wiped them away, struggling bravely to maintain her composure. Similarly, when Laura got angry, she hardly raised her voice, and never yelled; instead, she spoke in a monotone, explaining her anger rationally.

As Laura talked about herself, I could hear why therapy was frightening for her.

She said, "If I keep coming here and talking about all these feelings, we'll both be sorry."

"What do you mean?" I asked.

"Because I try really hard to be a polite person who doesn't hurt others, and to handle myself appropriately in any social situation. My mother was a very religious woman. She was always soft-spoken and in control. My skirts could never be too short, and my voice could never be too loud. When I was little, she told me if I used any curse words or did sexual things, I might not go to heaven. That really scared me. I learned to control myself and be proud of it."

"And what do you fear might happen if you lost that control?" I asked.

"I don't know exactly," she said. "But maybe if I start getting angry, I'll break all your windows or hurt someone—maybe even you. Sometimes I do get so mad inside, I think of hurting people, but that's not me, so I push those thoughts away. I feel guilty when I think like that."

I explained, "Anger, when it's not allowed to be expressed, builds. The desire to hurt, even to kill people, occurs when unexpressed anger builds into rage. Its intensity feels dangerous and overwhelming."

Laura's overcontrolled inner child was rightfully enraged at the stifling she had endured. She felt murderous, but could not accept that feeling as part of her ladylike identity. My reassurance and explanation helped a little, but she had to experience the fact that *feeling* out of control didn't necessarily lead to *acting* out of control. Step by step, she allowed herself to express anger more openly, discovering how to let go of control *slowly*, in stages. Although the process was embarrassing for Laura, she was much less threatened once she realized control didn't have to be an all-or-nothing proposition. With practice, she was able to integrate anger into her personality, and express herself in a healthier, more vital and energetic way.

Fear of Embarrassment and Failure

Carl's biggest fear was to be seen by me or anyone else in a way that would make him, in his words, "look stupid." To him, all emotions were private, "dirty laundry" not to be aired in public. If by chance a feeling did escape his vigilant control, Carl was deeply humiliated.

"I think my parents believed emotions were an unfortunate part of life," he said. "They tried hard to hide feelings or at least to minimize them. Whenever I got upset about anything, I was sent to my room and told to stay there until I was 'presentable' again. The only exception was if I was physically hurt and crying. Then I wasn't sent to my room, but they still tried to make me get over it as quickly as possible. I've always dealt with my feelings alone. Just being in this office feels like a failure to me. It's so embarrassing to show myself to you. For you to *see* me going through this, it's just too much to take. It's mortifying."

Carl had a tough time at first. But as he revealed himself, little by little, he discovered he was not ridiculed by me, or punished or ostracized in any way. Each positive experience contributed to his increasing ability to reveal feelings in front of another without experiencing intense embarrassment. He began to learn that to be all of himself with others is not failure but success.

Fear of Going Crazy

As recently as fifty years ago, only people who were very ill emotionally were felt to need psychiatric help. Mental health practitioners were almost exclusively psychiatrists; patients were defined as "sick." Today, psychotherapy is practiced also by licensed psychologists and psychotherapists who are not medical doctors but who are trained to work with a wide range of emotional and behavioral problems. Not everyone is aware of this expansion, and so some people still associate therapy with insanity. There is fear in our culture of the stereotypical "crazy" person, and people avoid therapy for fear of being deemed crazy. But, as I have mentioned before, mental health is a continuum; we all have problems, and therapy can benefit all of us.

However, as therapy begins and memories and feelings rush in, especially if they are unclear, they are temporarily overwhelming, and the person feels emotionally out of control. This feeling, unfamiliar and unacceptable to most people, can make a person fear losing his or her grip on reality and actually going insane.

One woman, Marie, described her experience like this: "When I feel too much at once, and I can't make sense of it, I get desperate. It's like a hurricane or whirlpool inside my head. I'm afraid I'll just flip out completely."

"What would that actually mean?" I asked. "What would happen?"

"Oh, who knows! Maybe I'd run down the street screaming, and then you'd have to call people to come get me. They'd take me away to an institution. I'd be locked up and trapped, at the mercy of those people who wouldn't understand me."

As Marie's therapy progressed, it became clear why this particular fear was so real to her. She told the following story: "My mother was very sensitive and artistic, and easily upset. My father was more of a simple person, self-centered and crude. I don't know why they ever got together in the first place, but they did love each other, and had five kids, including me.

"We didn't have much money, so sometimes life got scary and hard. At those times, my father started staying out all night—probably drinking and being with other women. My mother would be heartbroken. She felt so deserted by him, and she just couldn't handle all of us alone. She panicked each time he left, thinking he might not come back. He always did, though, and he'd apologize and explain how he had to get out because he was so worried, and it was his way of coping with the stress.

"My mother would always forgive him and take him back, but after some years, she started getting really depressed. When he'd leave, she'd get hysterical trying to stop him, and after he left, she'd cry and cry. I'd wake up in the night and hear her crying. She'd sit in the living room, in the dark, for hours. One day she stopped doing things. Just stopped. She didn't clean house or even take a shower. She kept her bathrobe on all day and started looking awful. When any of us tried to talk to her, she just got angry and cried.

"It terrified me, and it hurt so bad to see her. I was only seven at the time. One day an ambulance parked in front of the house and people came to the door. I heard my father talk to them in a really low voice, and then they came in and took her with them to a hospital. At least that's where my father told us she went. She was gone for a long time. I visited her there a couple of times; she looked awful. It was a weird place that smelled bad and had weird people in it. I didn't like going there, but I missed my mom. One day she came home and we never said any more about it."

Marie hadn't ever spoken about the trauma of her mother's breakdown; she had never before had the chance to process the terror, pain, and shame that she and the whole family endured. So when she began talking about her own problems in our therapy sessions, the emerging feelings triggered the memory of what her mother went through. Marie feared the same thing happening to her—that she would ultimately have to be hospitalized.

Marie had the courage to go through the fear, and continued allowing herself to open up to all feelings, past and present. She did not "go crazy" or have to be institutionalized. Marie did not have to repeat her mother's life. The act of *dealing* with her problems and her feelings in therapy was the opportunity her mother never had, and that opportunity made the crucial difference.

Fear of Vulnerability

Being vulnerable, by definition, means being open to the possibility of being hurt. Naturally then, at times, this fear arises in everyone. In therapy, people often fear becoming vulnerable.

Eddie's story typifies this fear: "I'm not only the youngest of three boys, but my brothers were jocks, and I was never as large or as strong as they were. I tried to keep up with them, but I really couldn't. We were always having fights. When one of them hit me, I'd try to act as if I didn't care. At least I wanted to pretend I was as tough as they were, but they knew I was faking and it just got them going more. They'd keep insulting me and hitting me, until finally I'd give up and cry. *Then* they'd really pulverize me."

For Eddie, being vulnerable was definitely not safe. To him, showing honest emotions meant being "pulverized." Understandably, throughout his life he kept up his guard around people, especially men. Eventually the walls he built, in an attempt to stay safe, created his prison of isolation and loneliness. He came to therapy to find his way out of that prison, but it involved doing the very thing he wanted to avoid—being vulnerable.

He said, "I thought by coming to a woman therapist, I'd feel safe, but I don't. I probably feel better than I would with a man, but I still can't open up. It feels like if I do, you'll use it against me, just like my brothers did. I know in my head you probably won't, and you're here to help me, not hurt me, but I'm still scared."

Eddie tested me by sharing small, not-so-risky secrets about himself, and watching my response. He discovered that I didn't use his confidences against him, or hurt him when his guard was down. He also discovered that being vulnerable has a positive side—being able to experience softer feelings, and the riches of emotional connection that come with trust.

Fear of Losing Family Relationships

Opening up the Pandora's box of the past usually brings with it a feeling of doing something wrong. This fear is rooted in childhood, when we believed that Mom and Dad were the unquestioned authorities on everything. As dependent children, we need to believe in our protectors, even if they're not good protectors at all. Some parents teach their children to obey without question—restricting the children's right to protest, even punishing protest with violence. Clearly, it's not easy to reverse this teaching and learn to speak out against the wrongs of the past.

Furthermore, families who hide secrets from the world—covering up alcoholism, physical and sexual abuse, affairs—often instruct their children to never say a word to anyone outside the family. It's quite normal to experience fear and shame when attempting to share those long-hidden feelings and secrets.

Jackie's reaction was just that. When she first came to my office, she was overflowing with words and feelings about herself, her marriage, her children, her job. But, when the time came to link some of her current life problems to her past, she stopped in her tracks. She looked agitated, as if I had just cornered her, and she was trying desperately to figure a way out.

In subsequent sessions, her shame and fear slowly melted away as she spoke: "I'm afraid to talk about what it was like at home. Whenever things happened, my father would grab my arm, hold it really hard and say, 'Don't you ever tell anyone our business.' His eyes were so mean, I was terrified. Even though I know it's irrational, I feel something bad will happen to me if I tell. I think if he finds out, he'll hit me, or at least never talk to me again. But how could he find out, unless I tell him? It just seems, somehow, he'll *know*. It always seemed he knew everything when I was a kid, or so he wanted me to believe. I felt ashamed of what went on in our house, and I still do. Besides being scared to tell, I don't even want you to know. It's too embarrassing."

This mixture of fear and shame is very common. The threat of punishment for exposing the family to outsiders is etched in children's minds. The "no talk" rule is an important obstacle to work through and overcome. Fear of telling the truth is part of the more generalized, ongoing fear that abused children live with every day, and it keeps them silent, oppressed victims, even in adulthood.

After working through the fear of punishment, Jackie discovered another fear—of telling the truth—which involved her current relationship with her parents.

She explained, "Now I *want* to say things, but I still feel like I shouldn't, for a different reason. My parents are both living, but they're very old and frail. I really care about them and I don't want to hurt them."

"You don't have to tell *them*," I said. "You can just tell me."

"I know it doesn't make sense, but it feels like they'll be hurt anyway. Somehow I'm betraying them and their trust in me."

These feelings Jackie expressed run very deep. Even though she had been abused as a child, she still loved her parents, and didn't want to hurt them. But the act of holding on to the secrets was hurting *her*. To protect her parents, Jackie was again sacrificing her own needs. She was still in the role of the victim-child who *had* to do anything to protect the bond with her parents, to keep herself safe and retain their approval.

As we worked through her fear, Jackie realized the high price she had paid for preserving the image of her parents as beyond reproach. She also now understood how, as a child, she had felt protected by her parents even though they were abusive, and that her need for their protection was so strong that she paid any price, even denying her own pain and her own reality.

Jackie saw how she carried this pattern of *denial* into her relationship with her husband. Too often in her marriage, she would ignore or suppress her own needs and feelings in order to keep peace with her husband. That was one of the reasons she came to therapy; she was a passive people-pleaser at home, and it made her depressed and resentful. In therapy, she began to see how her pattern of denial originated in childhood, and that the only way out of it was to face the truth.

Jackie continued to struggle, "Well, what if I do start talking about my parents? Even if they never know what I say, *I'll* know. Maybe I'll be so angry at them, or so upset, that I won't be able to be around them. Maybe I'll hate them, and I don't want to hate them."

Jackie's fear is a realistic one. It is impossible to work through feelings from the past without some emotional carryover into present-day relationships, especially relationships with parents. But there are several ways to approach this delicate situation. Some people, like Jackie, don't want to threaten their current relationships with their parents while working on the past, so they choose temporarily to reduce contact with them. Detachment can also be achieved through an internal process of emotional withdrawal. The purpose of temporary detachment is to lessen involvement and intensity in order to avoid conflict.

Some people, instead of avoiding conflict, choose to challenge their parents by openly exposing the truths of the past. The consequence of this type of confrontation depends upon the individuals involved. Parents, when confronted, may become defensive, unable to empathize with their adult child's feelings or to admit any of their own mistakes. A defensive reaction re-creates the past in a painful way and the adult child feels abused again.

The defensive parent is in denial, refusing to be vulnerable, needing to hold on to the role of authority. Adult children, at this point, could choose to sever their relationship with one or both parents, or at least greatly reduce their emotional investment in the family. This is a sad outcome, but a necessary one for some people. In fact, "breaking up" with a parent can have a liberating effect, as it is an assertion by the adult child of his or her own reality, a validation of the right to be respected.

A third scenario is a rather progressive one. One or both parents, if emotionally healthy enough, when confronted in a loving way by the adult child in therapy, can rise to the challenge by opening their minds and hearts to the truth. Most people really want to preserve a loving bond with family members. When parents do listen to their child's story, even a little bit of understanding goes a long way in making the child feel heard and cared about deeply, perhaps for the first time. The *attempt* to understand and empathize is, in itself, validating. When I hear about a supportive interaction of this kind I am touched, because great courage and love has been demonstrated on both sides. People *can* change. And they do.

Fear of Emotional Pain

Since I've said so much already about this subject, I'll be brief here. Fear of pain occurs at every stage of therapy. Initially, people seek help to get *out* of pain, so they expect to begin feeling better right away. What they encounter, instead, is a temporary *accentuation* of pain, as it is brought out and released. The unexpected pain can be upsetting and frightening to some people. Others feel they've been misled in their expectations. In their fear or anger, some people give up. The important thing to understand here is that getting through it requires acceptance of the fact that one has to feel *more* pain before one can feel better.

Fear of Memories

We automatically suppress whatever is too much to tolerate or integrate. When the past comes back in therapy, two things can happen: First, some memories that have been totally forgotten may be difficult to face, especially incidents that were particularly cruel or abhorrent. Second, past recollections can be shocking when memories emerge quickly, as they sometimes do, and the associated feelings are intense.

We now have a name for the reappearance of suppressed trauma: Post-Traumatic Stress Disorder (P.T.S.D.). This term originally referred to the trauma of war, and is now expanded to include other types of trauma, including childhood abuse. Both the environment of war and an abusive home environment are terrifying and require a constant defense against unpredictable violent forces. There is no real protection available against those forces, and no relief from the terror and pain of them. The agony of physical and emotional violence is both endured and witnessed. The constant strain cannot be tolerated, so an automatic shutdown of feelings occurs. If the emotions have no opportunity to be processed, they emerge later in the form of nightmares, sudden panic attacks, outbursts of rage, periods of depression, and feelings of extreme isolation and alienation.

Symptoms of P.T.S.D. can occur spontaneously or in response to an external trigger that recalls the original trauma. The symptoms, calling attention to the long-suppressed past, can be frustrating, painful, confusing, and embarrassing. Once again, pain is signaling a problem. In therapy, the trauma can finally be processed and integrated, and the human psyche heals itself.

In the decision to stop fighting against those painful and humiliating feelings, the way to hope and joy is opened. While the growth process is upsetting, it is also kind. After each period of intensity, there is a period of calm—an emotional resting state where integration takes place. Anguish and longing are gradually replaced by a connection to the inner self, emotionally and spiritually. Fear is seen for what it is—evidence of our limited understanding.

We participate in our growth, but we cannot expect to control it. The source of the healing process is Nature, or God, which is greater than we are. The most we can do is participate, and *allow ourselves to be healed.*

CHAPTER 4

RESISTING CHANGE: FIGHT OR FLIGHT

Just as pain has its place and purpose in our lives, so does resistance. It's healthy—part of our natural instinct for self-preservation. Sometimes it helps us by leading us away from danger, or by making us fight back when appropriate. Other times, it seems to be just a nuisance, but we need to accept it as part of being human, and part of life. Gravity is a force of nature which we resist. Inertia and entropy are other forces in our world which work in opposition to growth and expansion. We accept these forces, and rather than seeing them as only problematic we use them as means of structuring and defining our existence. We push against the limits presented to us.

Resistance is the voice inside which says, "No. / I don't want to. / I can't. / I don't have to. / You can't make me. / Why should I?" We continually experience resistance throughout life. For example, going to work can be a trial. No matter how much you like your job, some days you just don't want to do it! You may feel tired or bored, or there's somewhere else you'd rather be. We resist because of our fears, our wishes, our laziness, our beliefs. Whatever seems too difficult, too unpleasant, or too uncomfortable, we resist.

Not only do we flee from what we *don't* want, but sometimes we fight off what we *do* want. It can be very confusing. How often have you started something (like planting a flower garden, for instance), felt very enthusiastic about it, only to discover that within a very short time your enthusiasm had changed to resentment? Your beloved creative flower garden had turned against you and become a burden. The garden example shows how resistance is exercised not only against outer demands or pressures but against inner ones as well. Our motivations are so complex that our desires compete with each other. Even activities we choose purely for fun can bring up resistance. Skiing, parasailing, rock climbing—recreation involving no work, no deadlines, no maintenance—all bring up resistance. Why? Because they need to be *learned*, and because they include an element of danger which frightens us.

Just as I've tried to show you that pain is not a mistake, we shouldn't judge our emotional resistance negatively either. Instead, we can view it as an integral part of the growth process—grist for our mill, and a source of information to us about ourselves. Although we all experience resistance, we each have our specific characteristics. Every person avoids some things but not others, and avoids in certain *ways* and not others. As we understand *what*, particularly, makes us want to fight or run away and what methods (of fighting or running) we choose, secrets of our deeper selves are revealed.

This chapter is about the natural resistance you can expect to encounter in therapy. I've already talked about those inner voices telling you why you shouldn't start therapy at all. But even after you've decided to begin, the voices don't stop arguing with you.

Dr. M. Scott Peck, in *The Road Less Traveled*, writes:

> The tendency to avoid challenge is so omnipresent in human beings that it can properly be considered a characteristic of human nature. But calling it natural does not mean it is essential or beneficial or unchangeable behavior. . . . Indeed, all self-discipline might be defined as teaching ourselves to do the unnatural. Another characteristic of human nature—perhaps the one that makes us most human—is our capacity to do the unnatural, to transcend and hence transform our own nature.
>
> No act is more unnatural, and hence more human, than the act of entering psychotherapy.

The following examples illustrate types of resistance experienced by clients of mine in therapy, particularly during the early stages, but they by no means exhaust the wide range of avoidance behaviors used by humans feeling threatened. The purpose of these examples is to help you be able to recognize resistance for what it is, and to expect it. It is hoped that by understanding the impulse to run away, the reasons for it, and the ways it manifests, you will be better able to accept it as part of the growth process.

1. Thinking

The mind may be our greatest problem-solving tool in life, but even the mind has its limits. When thinking becomes a way to avoid problems, rather than solve them, thinking has become resistance.

As Denise's therapy progressed, she began to feel a lot of grief and sadness about events of her past and present life. She had the impulse to cry, but like so many people, she was afraid of crying and ashamed of it. To defend against her tears—to resist them—she started analyzing: "Gosh, I feel so sad, I wonder why? Maybe it has to do with . . ." Every time she'd feel tears well up, she'd immediately switch into a questioning mode and her tears would dry up.

I've talked a lot about the necessity of understanding the past as a crucial element in change; however, analysis has its place, and is not always called for. Sometimes what's needed most is to experience pure feeling.

Clients, at moments of deep feeling, often ask me questions like, "So what should I *do*?" or "What do *you* think?" On the surface these may seem like perfectly ordinary questions, but they are actually attempts at jumping out of discomfort. The question "What should I do?" seeks a solution; while there may be a long-range solution we can work toward to solve a problem, *the only solution to pain is to let it be felt*. Each attempt to skip over it simply delays the process.

The question "What do *you* think?" is similar to Denise's self-analysis, but also attempts to bring me into the analytical mode, taking both of us away from the feelings at hand. My response to being questioned at those moments is to redirect the person back to feeling. While this may be frustrating to the questioner, I do it because I know that what's required is simply to allow the pain and discomfort to come in, as unpleasant as it may be, for a short time. It needs to be experienced in order to work through the problem.

Obsessive thinking is another kind of thinking that's used as resistance. An obsession is a preoccupation with something to the exclusion of everything else. That mode of thinking will break in on other thoughts, crowding them out. If the object of thought is something pleasant, and creates a happy feeling, obsessing about it is usually a self-tranquilizing technique, like a fantasy, a way to get through a tough period. In small doses it can be useful and healthy; as a full-time avoidance method it is more like a drug, used to escape reality. Most people recognize obsession as a familiar experience. Often we become obsessed with a problem that *seems* unsolvable. Problems are rarely unsolvable, but sometimes any solution found is painful and therefore is deemed undesirable as a solution. Obsessive thinking gives the *illusion* of working on the problem, when actually it is simply a way to delay taking action.

To use Denise's example again: Denise was in a painful relationship (relationships are a common area of obsessive thinking). Her lover was married and planned to stay married. Though he complained a lot about his marriage and his wife, when the subject of divorce came up, he pulled back. Denise knew in her heart she should leave, but she was emotionally attached. Even the thought of leaving was acutely painful. But the involvement was acutely painful, too—she hated being part of an infidelity. Staying in it hurt; leaving would hurt, too. There was no pleasant solution available.

Denise spent hours looking for a way out: "Maybe he'll change his mind if I'm just loving and patient and don't push him. Or maybe I should call his wife and tell her the truth. He'd be mad at first but then he'd thank me. I know he's just afraid to hurt her; he would really rather be with me." (Denise spent a lot of her time analyzing him and his motives.) "Or maybe *I'll* change in therapy, and his marriage won't bother me anymore." On and on she went.

The mental chatter of thinking blocks out the pain associated with the situation—temporarily. As soon as the chatter stops, the feeling returns, hence the necessity for the thinking to be continuous and obsessive. The driven, compulsive quality of speech associated with this pattern reflects the fear behind it. A person caught in obsession is on the run, and knows it. Slowing down or stopping would bring back the pain.

There is no way to "figure out" a feeling. Trying to figure out a feeling is really trying to figure *a way out* of it. Often, people who use this type of resistance come from very verbal or intellectually oriented families. Thinking is an attempt to maintain control in a situation that feels out of control. Denise's unconscious belief was, "If I can just figure this out, everything will be okay." Finally she had to stop thinking, and let the grief she felt come to the surface, and be released. Once she stopped resisting, Denise was able to work through her feelings about the relationship, let go of it, and move on to greater possibilities for herself.

2. *Shutting Down*

Shutdown is resistance; it means temporarily losing the ability to feel emotions and/or the ability to think. Shutting down may happen for an instant or a few hours. Shutdown can also become habitual, when a person goes through the motions of daily life without feeling. In certain situations the ability to temporarily suspend feeling is important as a form of self-defense, but like all defenses, if prolonged or used habitually, it can inhibit growth.

To illustrate the mechanism of shutdown, imagine you're doing some routine business in a bank. Suddenly, someone screams. You turn around and see a group of men with guns robbing the bank. In a split second, you think through escape options and realize there's no way out—you're terrified. The robbers shout instructions to lie on the floor and shut up. You're a hostage. For a while you continue to feel panicky, frantically thinking what to do. But there's a limit to the amount of stress our bodies can tolerate at any given time. Finally, out of exhaustion and the body's natural, self-preservation instinct, you begin to shut down. Your mind simply goes blank and becomes numb emotionally. You get through the trauma moment by moment, functioning on a more basic, instinctual level. In an emergency like this, the ability to shut down is necessary, and a welcome relief.

In other types of stressful situations, however, shutting down can ultimately be detrimental. For instance, in a family, conflicts arise and need resolution. If family members don't have the knowledge or skills to resolve conflicts, they may shut down instead. When a parent is shut down, children know it. You may have been raised in an emotionally shut-down environment. Ask yourself: "Was there a lot of tense silence? When someone asked, 'What's wrong?' was the answer, 'Nothing'? Did you sense an emotional undercurrent of unexpressed feelings?"

When we are shut down, we are also shut in—isolated and cut off from other people. Sometimes, after an upsetting event, a brief period of emotional withdrawal is necessary. If it becomes the norm, communication breaks down, and intimacy is lost.

In therapy, when strong feelings arise, shutdown can occur as a self-regulating device, a way to let emotion in, a little at a time, to avoid being overwhelmed. But for people who use shutdown habitually, it is an automatic response against any pain, anytime. And shutting down can become a way of resisting the therapy process. If you are a person who shuts down, in therapy you will learn how to open up again. You will learn to come out of the habit of withdrawing and go beyond what's safe and comfortable for you. Confronting resistance is a delicate process, because you are challenging behaviors that were once necessary for emotional survival.

Let's look at the example of Susan. Susan grew up in a shut-down family. Anytime things heated up between her parents, one or the other would say, "Let's just drop the subject," or, "You win!" or, "Go to hell!" and then leave the room. The discussion was closed.

Susan said: "After those fights, the air felt thick and oppressive. Conflict just hung there, but no one said anything about it. I always felt uneasy for hours, wondering what would happen next.

"Whenever *I* was upset about something my parents did, and tried to object, I would hear 'Don't talk back to me' or 'Go to your room.' I wouldn't just go to my room, I'd *run* to my room, and burst out crying when I got there. I'd feel so mad and confused, but all those feelings were bottled up and made me feel crazy. I finally figured out how to put the feelings away—make myself forget about them and get involved in something else."

Susan's method of forcing her feelings away was a good one at the time. She hadn't really forgotten them though; she had simply shut them down. In therapy, that mechanism revealed itself. When Susan began to feel any strong emotion, she'd change the subject. If she began to cry, the tears would evaporate as soon as she'd switch to a lighter mode. The same happened with anger, fear, and shame.

I pointed out the pattern to Susan, asking, "What happened to that feeling?"

She said, "It just disappeared, like it went back inside or something."

"Can you bring it back out?" I asked.

At first she couldn't, but after a while she could. In fact, in time she recognized the pattern herself.

She'd say, "Oh I just shut down again" or "I feel the tears [anger, fear, etc.] leaving. I know I want to run away from this feeling."

By becoming aware of her automatic defensive behavior, Susan was able to interrupt the pattern, sometimes reversing the shutdown and sometimes even stopping it just as it began. As soon as the mechanism was interrupted, feelings returned. In order to grow and change, Susan was willing to push beyond her former limits.

3. *Rationalizing*

To rationalize means to explain, or to give excuses for something. We rationalize all the time to cover up mistakes we've made, and to justify doing something we know is wrong. We offer these explanations to our bosses, our friends, our spouses, our families, and ourselves.

When we rationalize, we try to believe and make others believe the validity of our statements, but in our hearts we usually know we're not telling the truth. There's a little nagging feeling inside, an uneasiness, revealing that something just isn't right.

In therapy, rationalizing usually comes up when a person feels disappointed or afraid. For example, Daniel went through what he perceived to be a failure in his therapy. Initially he was very eager, opened up quickly, and worked through a lot of past pain. He saw his life change, as he felt more self-confident and able to take risks. He left a job he had hated for years, and soon found what appeared to be a much more satisfying one. About a month after beginning his new job, Daniel came into his session depressed, discouraged, and angry.

He shouted, "My new job stinks! It's no better than the old one. I'm quitting this stupid therapy because it doesn't work anyway."

Therapy doesn't progress in a totally linear fashion. There are periods of growth, and periods of integration that feel like plateaus. There are also times of upset, when a problem surfaces and it feels just as bad as it always has. This does not mean therapy isn't working, but it does feel confusing and disheartening.

Daniel's new job wasn't what he expected. His old belief was that no job could be good for him (that's why he stayed at the old one so long) and now he felt his belief confirmed. He immediately felt hopeless and wanted to rationalize quitting therapy because of it.

"Who cares," he said. "It's not important to be happy in a job; most people aren't." Daniel's words expressed his sense of failure and his fear that his life could never really get better. In order to defend against the pain of his feelings, he tried to find reasons to give up hope. If he stopped hoping, he wouldn't be disappointed again. If he stopped coming to therapy, it would be easier to stop hoping and resign himself to an unhappy fate.

From time to time, everyone in therapy feels that the process is too difficult, too long, or too confusing. Everyone has periods of wondering whether therapy is "worth it," and periods of thinking about quitting. Rather than making a hasty decision, careful evaluation and patience are important at these moments; the desire to quit may be resistance to the therapy.

Daniel did not quit. I pointed out to him that he had broken a very old pattern by leaving his job. Maybe his expectations of an immediate "happily ever after" were a little too high. Just because his first new job didn't pan out didn't mean no job ever would. Maybe he needed to try again.

4. Addictions

Addictive behavior as resistance is a vast subject that can't be thoroughly covered here. However, I'd like to give an example of how addiction can function as resistance to therapy.

Joe came to see me saying he was depressed and didn't know why. He began his therapy with commitment and great intensity. I was impressed by his interest in his own process, and his willingness to work hard between appointments, keeping a journal, meditating, and recording his dreams. He brought notes to sessions, and was very intent on making the most of every therapy hour.

After a relatively short time, his dedication paid off; images and feelings started to surface. Then a funny thing happened—Joe began missing sessions. He canceled the first time because of a work deadline. I asked him if he wanted to reschedule and, surprisingly, he said, "No." The next week he showed up but appeared distracted and anxious, and hadn't done any of his usual homework. When I asked him about this obvious change, he said he was just worried about making his deadline. Then he canceled another appointment, saying he had to work late and just couldn't get away. After three of these seemingly out-of-character occurrences, I questioned Joe more directly:

"You seem particularly absorbed in your work right now," I said. "Is this unusual for you?"

"Oh no," he answered. "I usually work fifty or sixty hours a week, and take work home on weekends."

"Do you enjoy working that much?" I asked.

"Well, I don't know if *enjoy* is the right word. I get the job done, though, and people admire and respect me for it. I guess I like that."

"Can you imagine what it would be like to work less?"

"I think I'd get restless and bored. My wife and kids would be happy, though. They're always asking me not to work so much."

As we progressed in exploring Joe's work habits and how they affected his life as a whole, it became clear he was a workaholic. Workaholism is one of the least acknowledged addictions in our society, and its destructive effects are widespread. Joe, like thousands of other workaholics, was so obsessed with his job that he had no time for his family or himself. It was only after his wife threatened to leave that he began to see his behavior and its consequences more clearly. Previously, when his wife had told him she felt unloved, he couldn't understand why. In Joe's eyes, his work was a *demonstration* of his love—after all, wasn't he doing it for them, to give them security and comfort? Why couldn't she see that, and appreciate it?

In fact, to Joe, work was about much more than security and comfort; it was a method of avoiding feelings. By overworking, Joe filled all his time and thoughts, leaving no room for feelings at all. Problems had arisen in his marriage, years before. The problems were frightening to him, and since he didn't know how to handle them, he just threw himself into his work. Trying to avoid problems, his addictive behavior simply made them worse. Joe admitted that he hadn't been feeling well physically. Naturally so, since he never exercised, and he drank coffee all day and cocktails late at night to wind down. "That's how it is in business," he said. And he was right. That's how many people live, and in our culture they are rewarded for it by promotions, salary increases, and prestige. Many employees are expected to give more than a portion of their time to their work; they're expected to give their lives to it. Workaholism, as an avenue of escape and a sole source of self-esteem, remains largely unexamined in our society.

When Joe first came to therapy, he had only *appeared* open and totally committed to his growth. Actually, what Joe had done unknowingly was switch his compulsive behavior from one arena to another. He had made therapy his "work." As long as he was in the early stage of this process, he was fine, but as soon as deeper feelings began to emerge, he ran away. To resist therapy, he went back to the original site of his workaholism—his office.

Generally speaking, *whatever people usually do to avoid problems in their lives, they will also do to avoid the pain stirred up in therapy.* Other common addictive behaviors are:

◇ Excessive TV watching
◇ Shopping binges
◇ Increased smoking
◇ Overeating
◇ Drug and alcohol abuse
◇ Compulsive cleaning
◇ Addictive sex, romance, and codependent relationships
◇ Constant activity of any kind, including exercising, socializing, telephoning

Sometimes it is difficult to recognize when these behaviors are actually functioning as resistance. For example, often when people get into an intense period of growth and upheaval in therapy, they will suddenly announce they have fallen in love and, shortly thereafter, quit therapy. Falling in love is experienced as "the answer," and all problems recede into the background. A complete diversion has taken place, unconsciously. Or sometimes a client will become involved in a chaotic, addictive relationship, and stay in therapy—shifting the focus away from the inner exploration to an obsession with the trials of the relationship—again a form of distraction and resistance.

Addictions involving sex, love, and relationships are similar to workaholism in that they are indirectly (or sometimes directly) encouraged in our society and, therefore, harder to spot as problematic. Compulsivity and drama in the area of romance is viewed as natural, not a problem. When it comes to sex and love, "the more the better" still seems to apply.

"People" addictions are similar to work addictions, because both love and work *are* parts of life which we need and want. Therefore, determining when the line is crossed from healthy to self-destructive love or work is a complex and individualized process. A helpful definition is found in *Leaving the Enchanted Forest*, by Stephanie Covington and Liana Beckett:

> The basic distinction is that in addiction the focus is on the significant other, to the detriment of yourself, not because you freely *choose* this, but because you are unable to say no to that person, being inordinately dependent and fearful of rejection and abandonment. One generic definition of addiction is the chronic neglect of yourself in favor of someone or something else.

Recovery from addictions is complex and individualized. Unlike recovery from alcoholism, which requires an absolute, once-and-for-all cessation of drinking, recovery from addictions to work or to people requires a *change in the way of relating* to work or people, rather than giving them up altogether. An inner shift of attitude is necessary such that the activity is no longer compulsive and out of control, and is no longer used as a means of escape or attempt to get "fixed." Instead of being self-destructive, love and work can then be self-affirming and life-enhancing.

All forms of resistance are natural. They are merely coping strategies, although sometimes quite unhealthy ones. When understood, resistance can be a valuable tool for self-knowledge and transformation. Accepting resistance, without guilt and shame, facilitates healing. Even though the urge to give up can be strong at times, ultimately the stronger urge is toward healing. Life prevails over death. Hope wants desperately to win out over resignation. If you can weather the difficult moments, you will find that they fade and are replaced by a renewed sense of progress, strength, and optimism.

CHAPTER 5

SHAME AND SELF-EXPOSURE IN THERAPY

To get an idea of what shame is like, imagine that you are wearing layers of clothing on a winter day. The outermost layer is a big heavy coat, covering most of your body. Under the coat are your sweater and pants, but only the collar of the sweater and the cuffs of the pants are showing, because the rest is covered by the coat. What you are wearing under the sweater and pants is totally hidden from view.

One way to understand feelings is to think of them like layers of clothing—some feelings, like overcoats, are totally visible, some are partially hidden, and some are totally covered up. Most people wear an overcoat feeling. Think of someone you know and see if you can come up with one feeling he or she "wears" a lot of the time. Cheerfulness? Melancholy? Anxiety? Anger? Your friends could probably do the same about you. The feeling we wear most, on the outside, is one aspect of who we are, but certainly not the whole picture. In fact, some people continually wear their overcoat appearances specifically to hide what's underneath! The outer layer serves as a front to the world. It helps us get along with people, while still protecting our more private selves. The sweater-and-pants layer of feelings is a little more honest and unguarded, and is shown only to certain people, like family and friends. The most intimate layer of feelings is kept private, to be seen by a select few, or a chosen special one. Some people keep their most intimate feelings from everyone.

In therapy, we take off those metaphoric layers of clothing, one by one. The coat is the easiest to see and to work with, because it's the biggest and it's on the outside. As feelings are processed, others arise. Shame is often the overcoat, acting like a heavy blanket, suppressing almost the whole personality.

Mark had shame written all over him when he first walked into my office. His shoulders slumped, his head hung down, and he was unable to make eye contact with me. As he spoke, he stared out the window, just occasionally glancing my way to be sure I was still listening. His clothing fit poorly, and it was obvious he didn't give much attention to his appearance. We immediately began talking about how embarrassed he felt. In his case, shame was the overcoat.

Sometimes shame isn't identified until much later. It can be one of the most hidden layers, taking time to reach. Hidden shame feels like a straitjacket—elongated sleeves crossing your arms and extending behind you, tied there. You can't move, you can hardly breathe. You're helpless, vulnerable, and humiliated. You can struggle all you want, but you just can't get free. The more you try, the more tangled, frustrated, and deeply ashamed you become.

Shame says: "I'm bad, unacceptable, rotten. Don't touch me, don't show me to anyone, don't look at me." It's an excruciating experience of being repulsive, disgusting, and beyond redemption.

Shame is more intense than embarrassment, and slightly different from guilt. Guilt refers to what we *do*, rather than who we *are*. When we do something wrong, we feel guilty about it, and may apologize and make restitution of some kind. Guilt usually has a cause-effect pattern of beginning, middle, and end, whereas shame is all-pervasive, leaving no recourse for action. When we feel ashamed of ourselves, we want to hide from the world. We even want to hide from ourselves because the self-rejection is so painful. No amount of reassurance from the outside will change the internal experience of unworthiness. Shame clings like sticky sap on a tree.

In therapy, shame is elusive and, therefore, difficult to heal. John Bradshaw says in *Healing the Shame That Binds You:*

> Toxic shame parades in many garbs and get-ups. It loves darkness and secretiveness. Toxic shame is so excruciating because it is the painful exposure of the believed failure of the self to the self. In toxic shame the self becomes an object of its own contempt, an object that can't be trusted. . . . Toxic shame is experienced as an inner torment, a sickness of the soul.
>
> There is shame about shame. People will readily admit guilt, hurt or fear before they will admit shame. Toxic shame is the feeling of being isolated and alone in a complete sense. A shame-based person is haunted by a feeling of absence and emptiness. . . .
>
> The shame-binding of feelings, needs, and natural instinctual drives is a key factor in changing healthy shame into toxic shame. *To be shame-bound means that whenever you feel any feeling, any need or any drive, you immediately feel ashamed.* The dynamic core of your human life is grounded in your feelings, your needs, and your drives. When these are bound by shame, you are shamed to the core.

For most of us, *some* feelings are shame-bound, but not all. Just which ones are depends again on social and familial influences. When a forbidden feeling starts to surface, shame is triggered simultaneously and attempts to pull the forbidden feeling back inside.

To clarify, let's look at a situation with Sandy, a woman in her first few months of therapy. One week, Sandy requested a last-minute time change for her next session. I was unable to accommodate the request. When she arrived at the time previously scheduled, she sat with her arms folded, looking sullen, saying nothing.

I said, "How are you doing today?"

Sandy answered, "Fine, I really don't know why I came. I don't have anything to talk about."

It was obvious to me that Sandy was angry about something, and I suspected it was about the time of the session. I gently alluded to the situation as I saw it, asking her if her behavior might be indicating anger at me.

"No," she replied, "I'm not angry at you. How could I be? I know you're busy and couldn't change the appointment. No big deal."

Meanwhile Sandy looked more and more aggravated, fidgety, and embarrassed. Then, suddenly, her face changed, her body relaxed, and she began to launch into a chatty conversation about a minor event at work. I accommodated her by discussing that topic, but I knew it was a diversion from the more difficult issue at hand—her anger at me. Shame had successfully subverted her expression of anger, which was suppressed, and she went on to lighter things.

After a few minutes I turned the conversation back to what had happened, saying, "Sandy, I noticed you changed the subject when I brought up your session time. I know you *said* it didn't bother you, but you *looked* really upset. Would it be okay with you to get angry at me out loud, if you did feel that way?"

She was silent for a long time, then said, "No, you're the boss, you make the rules. I just have to follow them."

From there, we explored the childhood sources of Sandy's attitude about anger. She said, "Whenever I'd start to get angry, my mother would say, 'Bad girl! Good girls don't talk to their parents that way. Be sweet now like a good girl.' I felt awful about what I had done, like I wanted to sink into the earth and disappear. It was so humiliating, especially when she'd say something like that in front of other people. And she *loved* to say stuff in front of other people."

Parents unfortunately use shame as a disciplinary device—a tool for control. And sometimes they use it as a means of teaching. Whatever the purpose, shaming children is much more debilitating than it is helpful.

Sandy described what getting angry was like for her now, "I almost never express anger," she said. "In fact, I don't even *feel* angry very often. I start to feel it, but then it shuts off. Or if I start to express it, I get scared, like I'm doing something wrong. Usually I think about the other person's side until I understand it. Then I'm not angry anymore."

She would make herself "understand" until she didn't feel anymore. Shaming not only suppresses the *expression* of a feeling, but also makes *experiencing* the feeling seem wrong. Sandy had a complex set of defenses against anger, including shutdown and rationalizing.

To make the situation worse, shame also turns on itself. Sandy put it like this, "I'm embarrassed to be here in the first place, having you scrutinize me. Now I find out I'm ashamed to be angry. I don't want to be ashamed to be angry. If I'm here to get help, and expressing feelings is the way to do it, I just want to express them. Now I can't even do that successfully. I'm ashamed that I'm ashamed!"

Shame is like a prison, but it's not the kind a person can break out of by force. The more we try to force shame out into the open, the farther inside it goes, running to deeper and deeper hiding places. Shame cannot be healed by ridicule or minimizing. The healing of shame comes through understanding its sources, and freeing the pain associated with it. In other words, allow shame to come out of hiding, but only in an environment that is accepting, safe, and loving. Shame does not respond to commands, nor does it emerge in the presence of pity. It requires a gentle, supportive, respectful presence.

As Sandy said, therapy brings a lot of shame to the surface—shame for being vulnerable in front of another person, shame for having and expressing specific feelings, and shame for being ashamed. But in therapy, shame can be healed.

Just as Sandy struggled with being angry, many other people feel ashamed about feelings revealed in therapy.

People feel shame for being:

in pain	weak	free
afraid	vulnerable	happy
sad	exposed	wild
lonely	imperfect	sexual
needy	a failure	passionate
in despair	helpless	sensual
guilty	different	ecstatic
ugly	hurt	"too much"
stupid	angry	excited

Did that third column surprise you? Shame and happiness are so closely linked in our society that we hardly question it. For the most part we are still driven by the work ethic, and "too much" leisure is seen as laziness or indulgence. The wildness that is part of our animal nature is branded as inappropriate, rude, or out of control. Passion is still confined to its acceptable outlets, while daily life requires conformity and restraint in terms of dress, language, manners, and time. Sexuality may be freer than it used to be, but what do promiscuity and pornography really say? I think they say we're still trying to break free of repressive, shame-based ideas lingering in our collective psyche. Comfort, joy, play, pleasure, and ecstasy are still not natural for many people.

In therapy, a client may be at a loss for words on a good day when nothing seems wrong. Alice was one of these. She'd say, "I feel like I'm wasting your time. I'm supposed to be here solving problems. Instead I feel good."

"There's nothing wrong with feeling good," I'd answer. "It's just as valuable as problem-solving. Maybe you'd like to share with me what's going on in your life right now that's making you happy."

Alice blushed, "Well, actually, I've met a new guy who I really like. We've gone out twice so far and had great times."

"That's wonderful! And you hesitated to tell me?"

"Yes, because I thought you'd say I was running away from my problems."

"Sometimes people do use relationships to run away from problems, but I don't think you'd be here today if that was your intention."

Alice's initial blushing and evasiveness tipped me off that beyond her fear of my judgment, she probably also felt shame. As we delved into her past, she revealed a history of struggle. Her family had been poor and her parents pushed her to work when she was still very young. Her father's favorite cliché was, "Idle hands are the devil's workshop." Alice didn't have much time for play.

She remembered a specific incident: "It was a Sunday morning, and we were all getting ready for church. We didn't have to work on Sundays, so it was my favorite day, and I was happy. My sister and I were supposed to be making our beds, but in the middle of it, we saw how the blankets could be made into a tent. We got so excited looking for things to hold up our tent, and to put inside our tent, that we forgot all about making the beds and going to church.

"My father came in and went crazy. He started yelling, 'What are you doing? You lazy, good-for-nothing girls are going to make us all late! Can't you even do a simple thing like make a bed when you're supposed to?' He went on and on.

"I felt so awful, I really got the message for sure. From then on, I was intimidated. I worked hard at my jobs and at school, I never complained, and I tried not to break any rules. I basically gave up on fun. Playing was something other people could do, not me."

Alice was crying as she realized the depth of this loss of enjoyment in her life. She had been forced, by shaming, to become a worker-bee, never swerving from the tasks at hand. When she did venture out to find a little pleasure, she immediately experienced shame along with it.

An aware therapist will be on the alert for signs of shame. Lowered eyes, blushing, meek tone of voice, excessive apologizing—all appear briefly and signal shame, then may disappear just as quickly. The client, ashamed of the signs, may try to deny them, but a sensitive therapist will coax the feeling out gradually, so it can be healed.

Is shame ever good? Does it have a purpose in our lives? Author John Bradshaw makes a distinction between "healthy" and "toxic" shame. Here is how he defines healthy shame in his book *Healing the Shame That Binds You*:

> Healthy shame keeps us grounded. It is a yellow light warning us that we are essentially limited. Healthy shame is the basic metaphysical boundary for human beings. It is the emotional energy which signals us that we are not God—that we have made and will make mistakes, that we need help. Healthy shame gives us permission to be human.
>
> Healthy shame is part of every human's personal power. It allows us to know our limits, and thus to use

> our energy more effectively. We have better direction when we know our limits. We do not waste ourselves on goals we cannot reach or on things we cannot change. Healthy shame allows our energy to be integrated rather than diffused.

Healthy shame is humility—a realistic acceptance of our place in the universe. We do not have complete control over ourselves or the world, because we are not our own creators, we are part of the creation. Our physical bodies demonstrate, through their vulnerability and mortality, our places in nature's cycle.

However, the healthy shame of our bodies is often magnified to an unhealthy level, through shaming of natural body processes and overemphasis on physical appearance. Tina is a good example of this problem. Tina is very attractive and accustomed to being noticed by men. She always dressed stylishly, and based a lot of her self-confidence on her looks. The first time she began to cry in a session, she fought to contain the tears.

I said, "Tina, you're so sad. Can you let yourself cry?"

She answered, crying and stopping at the same time, "No, I don't want to. I look too ugly when I cry."

This led us into an exploration of her appearance and how she felt unlovable if she wasn't pretty. Months later, she had begun to allow some tears. Once, when she was crying, I asked if she would like me to hold her.

More shame surfaced with her reply. "No, because I'm afraid I'll get mascara on your blouse, or maybe I have bad breath or something."

Her fear led us to an understanding of a deeper level of physical shame—fear of being offensive, shame for being a real person with a real body instead of just a beautiful object existing simply to please others. This toxic shame inhibits our capacity to experience the joys and pleasures of life. Toxic shame can be so pervasive that it totally blocks spontaneity. It can reduce a person's life to a small and meager existence, confined by imaginary walls.

The healing of shame in therapy involves identifying what is shameful to an individual, bringing out the feeling, and tracing its sources. We all share the effects of whatever is shamed in our culture. In addition, we each have specific, shame-bound areas, learned in our families of origin. What is shameful to one is not necessarily shameful to another.

I worked with a man named Jeremy who felt ashamed of his level of intelligence. He was quite bright, but never fully believed it.

He said, "My father used to play mind games with me. He'd ask me what I thought of something, and when I told him, he'd put me down for my ideas. He made me believe he always knew what I was thinking, and that scared me. He focused on my mistakes and never gave me credit for my accomplishments. In school, I had trouble reading out loud. It's no wonder—I was so scared I'd make a mistake. The kids always teased me. It was humiliating."

Jeremy frequently felt ashamed in our therapy work. Here's an example of how it would happen: He generally brought notes of what he wanted to talk about that day. Many people bring notes, or lists, or journals to help them remember to cover topics of importance to them. Bringing notes is fine, but not essential or necessary. A good therapist can lead a client into important areas, even if the client doesn't initiate the conversation.

One session, Jeremy had finished everything on his list. There was silence. He looked at me quickly, then looked away, began toying with the edge of his chair, tapped his feet, blushed, and smiled in an embarrassed way.

I asked, "Are you feeling nervous, Jeremy?"

"Yes," he replied, blushing.

I asked, "What's going on?"

Jeremy said, "I've run out of things to talk about."

I asked, "So is that upsetting to you?"

"Of course it is." Jeremy was getting angry at me for not understanding something so obvious to him.

I asked, "Why?"

He answered, "Because I'm paying you money to help me, and I can't think of anything to say! You must think I'm really stupid."

Actually I didn't think Jeremy was stupid at all. Silences are common in therapy. What happens in the silence is that shame has a chance to surface, and usually an explanation of the nature of the shame comes with it. From there, we can trace the causes to their source. Because of the power differential between therapist and client, the therapeutic environment is very conducive to bringing out shame. While the client is open and vulnerable, much like a child, the therapist reveals little personal information, much like a parent. This imbalance recreates feelings from the client's childhood. Although it is uncomfortable for the client, the situation actually provides an opportunity to heal old wounds.

Shame is not limited to a minority of our population. We are all subject to the shaming influences within our culture. The value we put on wealth, power, youth, and glamour sets us up to feel inadequate, disappointed, and ashamed. We have come to believe in an illusion that "having it all" is possible, that some people actually do have it all. By constantly competing and comparing ourselves to others, and by measuring against perfectionist standards, we become dissatisfied with who we are. By always attempting to get somewhere, by striving and failing to reach the illusory goals, we lose the ability to appreciate and enjoy our lives.

Once again we are attempting to deny the fact that we are imperfect, and that life includes pain as well as pleasure, mistakes as well as successes. Shame steals our joy and freedom, unless we have the courage to face it and expose it for the lie that it is. We are imperfect, but we are wonderful anyway. We must be able to believe in our individual specialness, value, and beauty, accept our needs and feelings, and allow them to be expressed naturally.

CHAPTER 6

BECOMING REAL: OPENING THE EMOTIONAL FLOODGATES

All of us, whether we want to admit it or not, care what others think of us. Some people resist following trends and don't like to be part of groups, but even individualists are concerned about the opinions of persons closest to them.

In childhood, acceptance and approval are even more important than in adulthood. Acceptance and approval are critical needs of children in the process of forming their identities and self-image, looking to family and friends for direction. Children learn *who they are*, and whether to feel good or bad about themselves, through the eyes of others. If children's expressions of feelings and spontaneous actions are met with love and guidance, if needs and talents are noticed and nurtured, children have a chance to grow into authentic, creative, emotionally healthy adults.

If, instead, parents' problems dominate the family, and parents relate to a child through controlling, intimidating, and shaming, something very different happens. A child gets the message that his or her real self is bad, shameful, not good enough. *Then a false self begins to form, in the attempt to find parental approval.* We've already covered how children learn to hold back feelings. Besides learning what not to do, they also learn what *to* do, in order to elicit positive responses or avoid negative ones. A split develops between the shamed, rejected, real self inside, and the outer personality seeking approval. This split is damaging and painful, causing the child to take on a role, while the true self is abandoned. Emotional and spiritual needs remain neglected. Of course, children don't have the ability to understand what is occurring; they simply adapt to circumstances.

As time passes, the false self, or role, becomes stronger and more developed, while the real self recedes further into the background until it becomes merely a shadow. You may recognize in yourself feelings of dissonance and alienation, related to this splitting process, but you may never have known the reasons for the distress. By now, you may have completely forgotten, or lost touch with, your real self. Sometimes people who are fully entrenched in a role have moments of clarity, when they realize they're in the wrong place—doing the wrong work, with the wrong person, living the wrong life. But usually those moments are brief, and there's an accompanying sense of being trapped, too far gone, helpless to change. These feelings of futility make the truth unwelcome, and drive it back underground again. Sometimes the only clues are physical symptoms, stress-related illnesses, or chronic depression or anxiety.

Alice Miller, in *The Drama of the Gifted Child*, writes:

> Depression can be understood as a sign of the loss of self, and consists of a denial of one's own emotional reactions and feelings. The denial begins in the service of an absolutely essential adaptation during childhood, to avoid losing the object's love.

Often when people come to therapy, they can't define a particular problem, only a vague unhappiness. Neither can they be specific about what they want to change. Of course they can't. How can you know what you really want or need if you've lost the connection to who you really are? Besides, you might be confused by the role you've learned to play, if you have become competent and successful in it. Ironically, the more successful we are in achieving the goals of our false selves, the farther away we are from satisfying our deeper needs.

There are many roles to play in life, and sometimes we overlap two or even three of them simultaneously. Or we may stay in one for a period of years, then switch to another. Following are four commonly quoted examples. The first is one of the most popular and well-accepted roles a person can play.

The Entertainer. My initial impression of John when he came to me for therapy was of a witty, charming, self-confident man. His attitude was light and humorous, even regarding his own problems. While very entertaining, this behavior seemed to clash with the seriousness of what he was telling me. When I cautiously pointed out the discrepancy he said:

"Well, hey, you're a 'shrink,' right? I can't get too deep here or you'll shrink me so much my clothes won't fit!"

Just like John to answer a confrontation about joking, with a joke. By making us both laugh, John was minimizing the importance of his problems and keeping himself removed from deeper feelings. But there was more to it than that—it made him happy to make me laugh; it made him feel good about himself.

People like John are a lot of fun to be around, because they can bring up everybody's mood and be the life of the party. But as John's therapist, I knew he needed more from me than just to be another appreciative audience. He needed me to see beyond the act to the real person behind the mask, a person who had some problems and was looking for help.

I started by bringing John back to the subject of the joking itself. "You really make me laugh," I said. "But I know that's not what you came here for. I wonder if the jokes are keeping us away from something else?"

"Let's hope so," John answered, smiling slightly. His eyes looked mischievous and challenging, like he was playing a game. John was letting me know *he* knew he was using humor as a way to avoid deeper feelings, and he wasn't about to drop it just because I had figured out his technique.

"Sounds like joking is a good protection for you," I ventured, not giving up, either. I knew that John's defense, like all defenses, was an important ally to him, and should be acknowledged.

He responded well to my understanding. "Yes, it gets me out of a lot of tough spots. It always has."

This last comment led us into a conversation about his childhood. He explained how he had been a joker all his life: "In my family there was always a lot of fighting. It usually started between my parents, but whoever else was around was brought into it, too. Pretty soon there'd be a whole roomful of yelling. My older sister would try to calm everyone down, reason with them. That didn't work too well, but sometimes if I made a joke, it took them by surprise and they'd lighten up. It was great the way they looked at me—like they were grateful for it. I had bailed them out. It made me feel good when I could do that."

John had developed the role of joker in his family, and the behavior had fulfilled a dual purpose: (1) it distracted everyone from conflict, so it avoided pain and (2) it was a source of pride to him that he could pull everyone out of a fight. His self-esteem was enhanced by their appreciation.

Because of the ongoing, unresolved conflict in John's family, nobody's real needs were ever met. Whatever guidance John needed and might have benefited from, he did not receive. What did develop, however, was his innate talent for humor. It was a successful mechanism for coping with constant pain and stress, and it gave him a "good-guy" identity. Everyone loves a clown.

In his adult life, John had become a full-time clown. He made his living as a stand-up comic, and was accomplished and prosperous. He had lots of friends, especially in the entertainment field, and they all enjoyed playing off each other's humor.

On the surface it all worked fine, but just as in his childhood, John's deeper feelings and needs were never acknowledged. He had no idea what was wrong.

"Nothing's wrong," he said. "My life is great—my marriage is great, I love my work, I have friends, I have plenty of money." He hung his head, looking sad and ashamed. "I'm just not happy and there's no reason for it. I feel guilty even coming here when other people have serious problems. I don't know what's the matter with me."

"Maybe there's more to you than being funny," I said. "Have you ever thought of that?"

"As a matter of fact, yes," John answered, suddenly sitting straighter in his chair, at the sound of my question. It obviously struck a chord. "Sometimes I get mad at people because I feel like they just want me around to make them laugh. They *expect* it of me and love me for it. Well, that's great, but what if I don't feel in the mood to joke one day? What then? Will they stop wanting me around, stop liking me? I feel obligated to be a certain way for them."

Subconsciously, John was also obligated to himself to maintain that image. Otherwise, he risked losing attention and love. He was trapped in his own role. The role was developed for a purpose in his family, but it restricted him to a narrow range of behavior in his entire adult life.

"Has anyone ever asked you *not* to joke?"

"No way," he said.

Ironically, when a person gets stuck in a role, other people seem to get stuck in it, too. You might know someone like John who jokes all the time, and there are moments when you wish the person would get *serious*. You're not always in the mood for jokes and, besides, you can't get very close to someone who's clowning. But have you ever talked about it to the person? Probably not. It's much too risky to confront someone like John on his behavior, especially when the behavior appears to be his "personality." And you might also hold back because you don't want to look like you're trying to stop the fun.

Truth is, if you did have the courage to confront John or someone like him, you might not get a great response, because he'd feel put down. The only way he knows to feel good about himself is through joking.

So John was caught in a no-win situation. He resented people for using him for entertainment and not seeing his deeper aspects. But, if he were challenged, he'd feel threatened.

I said, "So you're in a bind; you know only one way to relate to people, and that feels good, but it also feels bad. I can see why you're unhappy. Even though everything in your life *looks* right, you are operating on a superficial level. As long as your connections to people are only through humor, your deeper self is neglected and alone. Humor is great, but it's only one way of being with people. You need more."

John didn't make a joke at this point. He sat quietly, thinking.

I made a suggestion, "How about trying a little homework? When you feel the impulse to joke, try to hold it back and see what happens."

He agreed.

In subsequent sessions, John was distraught. He had diligently done his homework and felt awful. "I hate this," he said. "I feel invisible when I'm with people and not joking. I'm used to being the center of attention and now I'm not anymore. In fact I don't even feel peripheral, I feel left out, awkward, useless. I don't know what to say or how to talk. Everything seems stilted and flat. It's boring. My friends are asking, 'What's wrong, John?' What am I supposed to say? I'm sure they'd love to hear 'Oh, I've just decided to stop entertaining you for a while.' That'd go over great!"

John's upset was understandable—he was attempting to let go of his lifelong role. I asked, "What if you *did* tell them the truth about what you're doing?"

He answered, "Most of them just wouldn't get it. They've never been in therapy or anything."

"What's your worst fear with them?"

"That they won't like me anymore! They'll think I'm weird and they won't want me around if I'm not being funny. This feels like a sure way to lose friends."

John was struggling. He knew he wanted to change and give up his old behavior, but he was facing a big fear—losing approval. He was also facing something else: the old buried feelings, long covered by his "Entertainer" act, were now starting to surface.

When people give up a conditioned, automatic behavior, generally the first feeling they'll experience is *fear*. In John's case, he described himself as "invisible," "useless," "boring" among his friends, and afraid of losing them. He probably felt the same way as a child at home when his parents were fighting. He couldn't intervene and resolve their problems, so he was essentially a helpless, invisible outsider, constantly afraid of the family breaking up, leaving him alone.

Since children don't have an understanding of the adult world, their imaginations carry them to terrifying extremes. And, since they are totally dependent upon their parents, fear of the family breaking up is emotionally equivalent to the fear of dying. In therapy, these feelings can rush in with sudden intensity, whole and intact, as if the experience had occurred just weeks (instead of years) ago.

John was flooded with memories, and talked about them eagerly for many sessions. Although he felt very sad to remember the truth about his young life, he was also supremely interested in uncovering it. The sad, scared boy from the past was finally emerging from behind his mask of humor, and becoming real. John discovered that while his loneliness as an adult was painful, his loneliness as a child had been far worse.

Identifying the false self and taking off the mask is one of the most important breakthroughs in the therapy process. For some people the transition is sudden, for others more gradual. As the truth of what has happened becomes evident, feelings of rage, sorrow, regret, and fear all surface. There is a sense of loss at having been alienated from the deeper self for so long.

This breakthrough stage is tumultuous for two reasons: (1) when you drop the old behavior, you are thrust into the feelings of the past and (2) your real self emerges in an essentially childlike manner, due to its neglect since your actual childhood, when the false self took over.

To clarify, let's look at the story of Nicole, who took on another of the common roles children learn.

The Heroine/Hero. Nicole is a successful attorney with a busy practice. Besides her affluent and semi affluent clients, she also works with many people who are poor and unable to pay. She feels good about this contribution she makes to society, but works long hours to keep up. In her private life, Nicole is a good friend to many people, helps her lover, Helena, in business, and is available to her elderly parents for extra help whenever they need it.

Nicole came to therapy saying she felt anxious and chronically fatigued. She recently was having bouts of crying for no apparent reason. As soon as she described her daily life to me, it was obvious why she was tired. Being all things to all people is a never-ending job, but to her it was just normal.

When we delved into the origins of her "helper" identity, we discovered she came from a large family with little money, and learned early that the more she helped out the more approval and attention she got. By the time Nicole was twelve years old, she was working for people in the neighborhood, bringing the money home to her family. A few years later she was working a full-time job and going to school, becoming more and more crucial to the economy of the household.

Being indispensable to others became Nicole's identity, and she felt proud of it. However, the years of overworking began to wear her down, as did the ongoing neglect of her own needs for peace, privacy, and free time.

Recognizing the source of her heroine identity came easy to Nicole, and it was a great relief to her. She wanted to change but the process of shedding the old skin was a bit rougher. She said, "I want to slow down, I really do, but it's so upsetting. I didn't expect this. I keep dreaming about my childhood."

"Would you tell me one of the dreams?" I asked.

"Well, sure. I'm about four years old, and I'm in the apartment we lived in then, but everything's different. It's all broken and devastated, as if a bomb dropped or there was an earthquake or something. Everyone looks panicky but no one's doing anything. They're just standing around and my mother's crying."

"Are *you* in the dream?"

"Yes—it's a nightmare actually. I'm sitting in a chair, *tied up* and *gagged*, like you've seen in movies or on the news."

"Are you panicky, too?"

"Yes, but the worst part is I'm totally helpless. I can't do anything but sit there and watch, as it all falls apart."

I suggested to Nicole that the dream was revealing how she must have felt as a young child, before she became the rescuer and problem-solver of the family. It was precisely this feeling of helplessness, in the face of pain and chaos, that propelled her into the savior role. By working hard, she reduced the panic around her and earned some much-needed attention from her overburdened, overwhelmed mother.

The interpretation brought Nicole to tears. "Yes it's true," she said, "and I'm feeling the same way now as I try to stop helping so many people. It's like the nightmare—I feel their pain, and I feel so guilty and selfish and bad if I don't help them. And I'm scared that everything will fall apart."

When a strong connection to the past takes place, it's almost like reliving the experience. The circumstances of childhood are re-created until they're finally resolved. In Nicole's adult life, she was still surrounded by poor and needy people who leaned heavily on her. She had much more work to do than she could handle. Just as in childhood, her role far exceeded her capacity. Now, as then, *her* needs were totally eclipsed; no one, including her, noticed her needs or attempted to meet them.

As her eyes opened to the reality of her past and present life, she was shocked and afraid. She said, "No wonder I did what I did. There's so much pain around that I can't fix. I just kept trying and trying. As long as I worked, I had the feeling things would eventually be okay. I kept the pain at bay, so to speak. Now that I've stopped trying so hard, I see it just can't be done—I can't fix other people's lives. But it's so sad. I'm scared for everyone. I'm afraid they won't make it."

Reexperiencing the past, through similar circumstances in the present, brings the past back to life. While it can be shocking and painful, it is the vehicle for reconnecting to the traumatized child-self, the self who got lost along the way. It gives the true self an opportunity to emerge and be recognized.

In therapy, conceptualizing the real self as a hurt inner child is used to help clients understand the lost part of themselves. Creating a dialogue between the adult and child brings out the child's personality. At first, the appearance of the child-self is like a rebirth, an awakening of a forgotten, or almost forgotten, being. As false-self behavior diminishes, more and more space for the real self is created. However, the real self is unformed, undeveloped—naturally so, as it's been buried since childhood. The "inner child" emerges as any child would—vulnerable, curious, and spontaneous. Behavior and feelings are unpredictable.

Here's an example of Nicole's dialogue with her inner child in a therapy session. The purpose of this particular conversation was to give the child a chance to speak without being criticized. The therapeutic environment helps clarify the ongoing conversations we have within us, usually outside of our awareness. The child's voice is most often drowned out by the role-playing adult trying to survive.

ADULT: What do you want?

CHILD: [cries immediately] I want you to stop pushing me around so much. I want to go out and play. I'm lonely. It's too sad.

ADULT: But I told you before, we can't go out and play because everybody needs us to work. We have jobs to do.

CHILD: But I'm tired of it. Forget everybody.

ADULT: Oh no, I can't do that. I'm too afraid. Everything would go crazy.

CHILD: But I don't care! [angry now] I want to go out and play! You don't love me! You don't care about what I want!

Through dialogue, Nicole learned that her inner child was a real part of herself who deserved attention and respect. She resolved to change her behavior. As Nicole began to let go of being the heroine, she found herself confused about how to behave. Like John, she felt out of place, awkward with people. She was afraid no one would like her if she wasn't helping them. In social situations she often didn't know what to say. To Nicole, this new, shy personality was very uncomfortable—she thought she was losing ground, getting worse instead of better.

I told her, "Therapy is not a straight-ahead process. It goes up and down, back and forth. Think of it like riding a bicycle—your feet on the pedals are sometimes going forward, sometimes going backward, but always going in circles; nevertheless *you* move forward. Your real self has to catch up with you. She has to learn about the world and you have to learn who she is."

At this point in therapy, aspects of the personality, suppressed in childhood, can be expected to come forward. If you've been like Nicole, a hard-working heroine or hero, and now uncover the repressed child in you, you'll probably go to the other extreme—do exactly what you want, be totally self-centered. You'll feel like quitting your job (or at least leaving early), and going out to play. You might also find yourself saying or doing things that seem out of character for you. They *are* out of character for your adult role, but not at all for your inner child.

Nicole came to my office one day, upset, saying, "You won't believe how I've been acting. I'm so embarrassed. All of a sudden, in the middle of a conversation with some of the other attorneys in my firm, I started getting real silly! I was giggling about nothing and teasing one of the men. They looked at me like they couldn't believe it. Then I joked about a case we were working on, and they rolled their eyes at me!"

I assured her that what she was going through was natural.

"That's not all," she wailed, exasperated with herself. "You know I never lose my temper with people, and all of a sudden I'm snappy and irritable. I feel like telling people to 'get with it' and do their share, instead of leaving it all to me."

"Sounds like what you might have been feeling for a long time," I answered. "People have always left too much for you to do, and you're finally getting mad about it. That anger has been waiting for an opportunity to express itself.

"It's important to allow yourself the freedom to be less controlled than usual, at this time," I told her. "Your behavior may be childlike and cause you some embarrassment, but it's a very real expression of who you are. Don't shame or suppress yourself. If you do, you'll be giving yourself the same message your parents gave you. Be as patient and loving as you can, no matter what you do. Indulge yourself."

"Indulge yourself" is a foreign concept to Nicole, and to most other people as well. I don't mean to indulge to the point of recklessness or excess which could be destructive. I simply mean be generous with your deprived child-self. You've lived long enough in your role, and role behavior is not self-nurturing (even though it attempts to be).

There are two more roles commonly played. Both of these *appear* to be more self-nurturing because they're not oriented toward people-pleasing, as are the Entertainer and the Heroine/Hero. Actually, they are no different than the joker or the heroine/hero in their failure to meet deeper needs.

The Loner. In an earlier chapter I talked about Gene, who as a boy in a chaotic family attempted to console himself by going to his room and playing ritualistically with his toys. The loner avoids people because people can cause pain. Gene learned to stay out of the way, believing that his presence created problems. With his family, that behavior protected him, but in the outside world as an adult, it isolated him. Gene was unable to make friends or take part in any social activity unless he went by himself, and stayed by himself.

Loners are masters at withholding. When faced with any kind of confrontation, they tend to withdraw and show little or no emotion. This can be exceptionally frustrating for someone who is trying to engage in an argument. It's like hitting a ball against a curtain. Like all other adaptations, the loner's tactics were learned in response to painful and threatening conditions in childhood. By withdrawing emotion, the loner is saying, "I won't give you anything, not even my anger. I won't show you that you bothered me at all." Hiding the hurt is a last-ditch effort to preserve some shred of power and dignity, attempting to avoid humiliation and total defeat. This defense often occurs in families where parents are abusive, and who become *more* abusive when the child cries or demonstrates fear or anger.

Loners often become addicted to overeating, alcohol, drugs, or (like Gene) ritualistic behavior. All these behaviors are attempts at soothing the pain of loneliness and minimizing fear of being alone in a hostile world. Since loners are fundamentally afraid to trust people, they can't allow themselves to be vulnerable to others helping them. Therefore, they try to comfort themselves by whatever means they can, falling into traps of addiction.

Changing his loner "behavior" was an act of great courage for Gene. He had to inch his way closer to people, frequently going back into solitude to recover his sense of security. He had to be willing to talk, reveal himself, even though it felt so risky. The rewards were great for him; for the first time in his life he had the opportunity to experience real friendship and intimacy.

He said, "I never knew what I was missing before. I prided myself on not needing anyone, but now I see how good it feels to let people know me. I'm still afraid that if they *really* know me, they'll hurt me, or at least not like me, but I also know those are just fears coming from the 'old me.' I'm letting people in more and more, and so far no one has run away or hurt me."

Becoming real is a challenge. Giving up a lifelong role is a type of death, so of course there is a fear in letting go. Since the new self doesn't form overnight, the interim period is disturbing in its lack of definition. It feels a little like "being no one"—like having no real identity—and it feels like it will go on forever, but it doesn't.

The Scapegoat. This is the child (later teenager and adult) who rebels, displays anger and violence, breaks rules, and generally gets in trouble. The role got its name because the child who acts in this way is generally the focus of blame for all problems of the family. In actuality, rebellious behavior is a *response* to the family's problems: It can be a demonstration of pain from being neglected, an attempt to get attention, and a reflection of a situation in the home.

For the scapegoat, becoming real requires almost a reversal from a negative, destructive direction to a positive, constructive one. By the time a scapegoat becomes an adult, he or she may have a history of addiction, irresponsibility, or crime. While on the surface there may be bravado and pride about this role, underneath a scapegoat feels shame, pain, fear, and rage.

Al described his transition from addiction and crime to recovery: "It's not just that I have to stop doing certain things, and acting certain ways, I have to change my whole life! Almost all the people I hang around with are strung out on something, and a lot of them have done time in jail. Most of the money I've made has been on the illegal side. Now I've got to go straight! Truth is, I want to go straight, but I don't have any idea what to do, or who to do it with."

Al wasn't exaggerating—he *did* have to change his whole life and it wasn't an overnight process. At first he felt slow and "square," and he had a tough time saying good-bye to his friends. But, as he processed the events of his childhood and began to understand the more hidden depths of himself, the changes became easier. He realized that what he was letting go of wasn't so good after all.

"Being 'bad' was okay," he said, "but in a way it wasn't that great either. When I was a kid I used to set fires. It made me feel powerful, like 'now I showed them!' But actually they didn't even try to understand what I was doing. I was so angry and hurt, and all they did was punish me. I just got more hurt and more angry. Nobody ever asked me why I did it or what was wrong with me. When I grew up, it wasn't much different. All the guys I hung with were on their own trips, getting out their own anger, or trying to stay high all the time. We were buddies, but looking back I see that we weren't really close friends—no one ever let their guard down enough. So in a way, it's good I'm cutting them loose."

As Al got closer to his real feelings and needs, his old associates weren't enough for him anymore. Even though it can be hard to leave a social circle and form a new one, many people need to do it. Most alcoholics and addicts in recovery have to make new friends in order to stay sober, because they can't be around people who drink and use drugs.

The bottom line is, when you change yourself, your life changes around you. You feel, act, and see things differently. You want different things. Initially the transition is awkward and embarrassing, but in the long run it smooths out. Fears of losing friends or jobs are usually not substantiated, but, as in Al's case, sometimes old friends do drift away (or you choose to leave them) simply because you don't have much in common anymore.

Nicole, on the other hand, didn't need to end any of her personal relationships, but instead she deepened them. Nicole learned that while people gladly accepted her self-sacrificing assistance, they did not reject her when she withdrew just enough to take care of herself. When she became less of a perfectionist in her work, reduced her client load, and began joking more with her co-workers, she was not fired. No one had expected her to do so much work in the first place—she had been her own worst enemy.

About her relationship with her lover she said, "When we were together and the 'inner child' of mine started coming out, I was really scared. I snapped at Helena, had little tantrums, then I'd burst into tears. Sometimes I'd get real sexy, but in a teenage, teasing sort of way. She was surprised, but no one was more surprised than I was. I've *never* acted that way before. Tantrums? Me? No. Being sexually provocative? No way. But I tried to do what you suggested—to remember that a long-buried part of myself was surfacing. I thought: 'If a real child was kept locked up for years and then released, of course she would be bursting with energy and feelings, and at first she'd be wild.' I told myself it was just temporary, and it was, the really wild, uncontrolled part at least, but some of it has stayed. And you know what? I like it. And so does Helena. She was confused at first and got a little hurt, but as I explained it all to her, she began to understand. Now she confesses that she really likes the new me *better than the old*. She thinks I'm more fun than I was before. She's right."

In John's case, his transition from full-time entertainer wasn't as extreme as Nicole's. He didn't want to change professions. His childhood had trained him well to be a comic and he enjoyed it. In fact, he even incorporated some jokes about the therapy process into his routine. He did make some changes in his personal life though. While he kept the friends he "bantered" with, they became less central.

He said, "I think of it like this—I'm in the center and there are all these circles around me. In the past, my 'jokester' buddies were the closest circle to me. Now I've moved them to an outer circle. I'm making some new friends to be in my inner circle—people I can really talk to. And I've gotten through to my family, too. For the first time, I'm trying to talk seriously with my parents and my brothers and sister. They say they don't recognize me, which is great, because it means I *am* really changing, and that's what I want. I could tell they didn't like it too much when I started to change. They're used to me always kidding. And at first I got too serious—went the other way. Slowly, I'm finding a middle ground where I can joke sometimes, and sometimes be serious. It's a good feeling."

What John described can be referred to as finding the gray area between the extremes of black and white. The role learned as a child was essential then, and is still useful now. Becoming real doesn't mean totally dropping the familiar personality. John's humor continued to bring him success and popularity, but it no longer restricted him to superficial relationships. He controlled *it*, instead of it controlling him. He used it when he wanted to, and not when he didn't.

Nicole's competence and her sensitivity to the feelings of others are valuable qualities. Once she learned to take care of herself too, Nicole led a balanced life as an excellent attorney, and a loving relative and friend.

Al's ability to express anger and go against conventional rules had gotten him into trouble, but also contributed to his healthy individuality. He knew how to lead instead of always following, and he wasn't afraid of people. Integrating those traits into a sober, legal lifestyle was the challenge for him.

In conclusion, becoming real requires, first of all, the recognition that we play roles much of the time. Second, it requires understanding that, although the behaviors we learned as children were useful and necessary in the past, they become a hindrance in adulthood if they restrict us to a narrow range of experience. Third, to become real demands the courage to act in ways contrary to what was learned, allowing new feelings and behaviors to emerge. It includes tolerating an unpredictable, emotionally volatile period, seemingly irrational outbursts of tears, or inappropriate actions. It means accepting all feelings and behavior, not without some restraint, but with compassion for the deeper self who is finally allowed to come out. And last, it means being willing to live through a time of uncertainty—a time of not knowing exactly who we are or where we're going—a surrender that may bring fear, despair, and darkness, but which is truly the breakdown before the *breakthrough*, the darkness before the dawn.

CHAPTER 7

FROM DESPAIR TO HOPE

Despair is not a popular or welcome word in our vocabulary. Maybe we believe that if we just don't say it, it won't exist. A scary word, it's threatening because it refers to an emotional state we never want to be in, and would prefer not to think about.

Despair feels hopeless. It can shriek, moan, cry, or be silent as stone. It's the furthest extreme of sorrow and suffering, and can vary from excruciatingly painful to dull and numbing.

Sometimes people come to therapy because they're in despair, finally driven to seek help after exhausting all other attempts. For others, despair is part of the therapy itself, experienced when a stark truth is acknowledged, or a defense against feelings is relinquished. The process of becoming real—letting go of conditioned behavior—as described in the prior chapter usually brings some despair. The pain comes from making contact with the lost self of childhood, realizing the split between the authentic self and the role-self, and feeling at a loss regarding the future. A great chasm appears to exist between the known past and the potential ahead, with no road map showing how to proceed.

We want to resist despairing; to some people it feels like a defeat—shameful—as if we are supposed to be able to solve every problem, overcome any hardship, or better yet prevent them from occurring in the first place. The truth is, we have no control over much of life, and certainly as children we have less than we do as adults. Despair is humbling, but we don't always want to be humbled. We have a hard time facing our own limitations.

Let's take another look at Al, the man who gave up drugs, drinking, and crime to start life over with the help of recovery programs and therapy. Although he saw the benefit of his choice to change, and intellectually understood the difficult nature of it, Al could not have been prepared for what happened to him emotionally during the change process.

After a few months he was ready to give up and go back to his old lifestyle. He said, "This is impossible; I can't change. It's too late for me. I'm too old, too much water under the bridge. I've wrecked my life, let's face it. I'll never be able to stay sober, find new work, make new friends. Forget it, it's too much."

Al fell silent, staring out the window. His eyes were dark and glaring. The scowl on his face and the smoldering fire in his eyes let me know he was feeling not only despair but rage.

I said, "You sound like you feel hopeless, and angry too."

He burst out, "Well, wouldn't you be? Yes I'm mad, I'm furious! Do you know how frustrating it is to be one way your whole life and then find out you can't be that way anymore? I'm sick of being drunk, sick of jail, sick of everything, but that's who I am, and I might as well accept it. I'm just a bad apple and that's the way it's going to be."

Al's rage was an expression of the overwhelming tension and frustration he was feeling, caught between an outworn old self and an unborn new one. He was pulled back to the old, the known, the predictable—something he could count on—but it was distasteful now. On the other hand, the prospect of starting over seemed impossible. Al was desperate as he struggled, unable to move. He was unaccustomed to feeling pain and confusion of this nature.

I said, "Well, if you did go back to your old lifestyle, it would get you out of this intolerable tension, wouldn't it?"

"You're damned right it would!"

"But you don't really want to do it?"

"No." The sadness of despair was showing on his face now. "I don't know what to do. I wish I had never been born."

I knew I couldn't console Al. There is no real consolation in despair, except the caring presence of another person. No pat formulas or words of wisdom can fix a situation that requires time to resolve itself. Any glib answers I could have given would have been met only with resentment, and I knew it. All I could do for Al at that time was to let him know I understood what he was going through, and how hard it was for him. And, that although he felt hopeless, *I* had hope. I had seen many people make it through the pain he was suffering, and bit by bit grow into the new persons they wanted to become.

"It takes time to grow," I told him, "and growing isn't always easy. We can water a plant and put it in the sun, but we don't *make* it grow. We *participate* in our growth, but nature, or God, or whatever the energy of creation is, does the rest."

"God!" he barked at me. "Don't talk to me about God!" (Apparently my plant metaphor had sounded like a pat answer to him, and he was angry.)

"Why not?" I asked.

"It's obvious there is no God, or if there is, He doesn't care a bit about me. All I've ever gotten is the short end of the stick my whole life. I got beat up by my parents, then my teachers, then the law. Now I'm trying to go straight and I'm getting more beat up. Don't talk to me about God. I used to believe in God but I don't anymore."

It was clear that Al was disillusioned; he wanted to hold on to the faith he once had, but he couldn't. His faith could not withstand the trials he had been going through. He was angry at himself, at me, at life, and at God. Most people don't have the nerve to express rage at God like Al did, but many feel it nonetheless. When circumstances don't adhere to our concept of fairness, or follow our timetable, we feel betrayed. Where is God when we need help? What about all those religious promises about God's love?

The truth is, we aren't capable of comprehending the spiritual dimension of the universe, not with our rational minds, anyway. But we carry around our own personal concept of what God is; that's the best we can do. So, for most people, when life doesn't follow a logical pattern, we feel despair and we fear that something's wrong—maybe God doesn't exist, or has forgotten us, or is punishing us, or just isn't so loving after all; or maybe there's a force of evil (Satan) who works against God.

There's a Buddhist saying: "Paradox and Confusion are Guardians of the Truth." I interpret this to mean that if we attempt to reach an understanding of the truth of existence, through thinking, we get no farther than the two Guardians. We are left with the confusion of paradox—realities that seem to conflict: riches vs. poverty, abundant creation vs. natural disaster, health vs. disease, love vs. hate, pleasure vs. pain, compassion vs. cruelty, achievement vs. destruction. We'd prefer to believe in a God who conforms to our desires for justice and goodness. It's not easy to have faith in the face of sorrow we don't understand.

Alan Jones says in *Soulmaking:*

> Our idealization about God is like "falling in love." We become disillusioned as we find out that God is not as we thought—God is not just peace, love, harmony, ease—or at least not for us. God always demands of us, more than we think we want to give. . . .

> The soul . . . is a movement that begins whenever man experiences the psychological pain of contradiction. . . .
>
> The task of the believer is to contain the energy of The Question within oneself. . . .
>
> We need to help each other. Without help I get trapped inside myself, and the pain of contradiction is translated as despair because I don't know how to interpret what is happening to me.

In other words, true faith means having a spiritual vision that *includes* and *goes beyond* the polarities of what we call good and evil, even though we don't understand them. It means allowing for the possibility that what we call God may be bigger than all of our attempts to make sense of things, and that we have no way to verify any of our guesses. Having faith, as I see it, is a *choice* based not on external proof (for a case can be made for any point of view), but on an inner certainty or intuition, mixed with hope. Some people have it all their lives; some develop it; some people don't have it but wish they did; others don't have it and don't want it. It's one of the most personal, individual attitudes in life. As a therapist, I don't attempt to sway people toward any view; I work within each person's own view. If their belief works well for them, fine; if their life is not going the way they want, and they've tried everything else, I'll suggest looking at the spiritual side.

Some people, like Al, do have a spiritual belief but have lost faith temporarily through the disillusionment brought on by difficult circumstances. In those cases I try to act as a lifeline—someone to hold on to, who represents the lost hope and who can see the light at the end of the tunnel. I share my own faith, my own experiences, and any religious metaphors I can think of, to remind the person that it's human to give up at times, and that he or she is not alone. Despair is just another part of life, another feeling, another experience to pass through.

The story "Footprints" is a touching and reassuring expression of faith found in despair:

> One night a man had a dream. He dreamed he was walking along the beach with the Lord. Across the sky flashed scenes from his life. For each scene, he noticed two sets of footprints in the sand; one belonging to him, and the other to the Lord.
>
> When the last scene of his life flashed before him, he looked back at the footprints in the sand. He noticed that many times along the path of his life there was only one set of footprints. He also noticed that it happened at the very lowest and saddest times in his life.
>
> This really bothered him and he questioned the Lord about it. "Lord, You said that once I decided to follow You, You'd walk with me all the way. But I have noticed that during the most troublesome times in my life, there is only one set of footprints. I don't understand why when I needed You the most You would leave me."
>
> The Lord replied, "My precious, precious child, I love you and I would never leave you. During your times of trial and suffering, when you see only one set of foot-prints, it was then that I carried you."
>
> Author unknown

But what about people who are not spiritually oriented, and not interested in developing faith? Getting through despair without any spiritual belief is difficult, but not impossible.

Marlene was raised by atheistic parents who taught her that all religions were lies based on the false hopes of weak people. They told her to count only on herself.

Marlene was in deep despair when she came to see me. She had been unhappy for years and unable to pull herself out of it.

Counting only on herself just wasn't working. Sounding very ashamed, she said, "I just don't want to live anymore. Nothing's right. I'm so lonely. I haven't been in a relationship for six years. I don't have any friends, my job is awful, and it doesn't pay enough money. I'm nowhere and going nowhere." Although Marlene was staring hard at the floor, trying not to cry, tears were beginning to show. "If I had the courage, I'd kill myself, but I don't. You know what really stops me? My parents. They always said success in life is all up to me. Suicide would be a failure in their eyes, and somehow I just don't want to be seen as a failure."

"Would you see yourself as a failure if you gave up?" I asked.

"I already see myself that way," she answered, crying openly now. "Do you know how hard it was for me to come here? Just being here means I couldn't make it on my own."

"Well I'm glad you did come here," I said. "Especially since it was so hard for you. None of us can make it totally on our own. We all need each other's help."

"I'm afraid you can't help me either," Marlene whispered. "No one can."

In the sessions that followed, Marlene cried a lot of tears. Years of loneliness poured out as she talked about her life. As a child, she had felt terribly abandoned and afraid. The kind of strength and independence her parents demanded weighed heavily on her. By the age of three she had rashes on her skin from anxiety. Although her parents were attempting to prepare Marlene for success, they actually set her up for defeat. By teaching such extreme independence, they denied her access to any emotional support or intimate connection with people. Relying only on herself left her stranded; there was nowhere to turn—not to people, not to God. For Marlene, coming to therapy was a desperate measure, undertaken with a very pessimistic outlook.

During the first few weeks, her despair deepened as she fully acknowledged the extent of her pain and her belief that there was no way out. She felt lost, and she continued to think about suicide. "I just don't want to be alone another day. I don't want this life. Why is it like this? What's wrong with me? There must be something I should be doing but I don't know what it is. If I can't figure it out, nothing will change. It will be like this forever and I can't bear it. I'd rather die."

When despair doesn't lift quickly, thoughts of suicide can enter in. Not all people consider suicide, but many do. Some individuals are horrified by the mention of the word, and don't allow themselves to think of it. For others, thinking of suicide is a comfort—a last effort at controlling a life that feels out of control. If pain hurts too much for too long, at least death provides the promise of a way out.

Perhaps the most devastating aspect of despair is the way it distorts our perceptions. Suddenly nothing seems real but the darkness, which appears to extend in all directions. The future lies ahead with doomed certainty. There's a heaviness that never lifts, and a fatigue to the bone. Never mind that in reality everything *could* change—to the person in despair, good news belongs to someone else. Despair feels irreversible, permanently empty, and intolerably lonely.

I told Marlene I understood how she felt. I did not try to do anything more than to give her my support and empathy. Unlike Al, Marlene was not looking for faith to pull her through. She was simply drowning. However, I knew by her presence in my office that Marlene still wanted to live. And I believed that what was necessary for her to make it had already been accomplished. She had, by turning to me for help, broken the rule of her life, the rule that had trapped her: "Count only on yourself." She was now experiencing the grief that living by that rule had caused her. What she didn't know, and couldn't see in her despair, was that by letting in the truth, and accepting it, she was actually going to find her way out of it. But she had to wait.

It's not easy to go through despair as Marlene did. As a therapist, it's painful for me to watch a person suffer so much. It's tempting to offer reassurance or solutions, but solutions feel trivial to someone in despair, invalidating the all-encompassing magnitude of the experience. Empathy is important, but not pity. Even a person who is self-pitying does not want to be pitied; it's perceived as a put-down, shaming.

In fact, I admired Marlene for having the courage to go through her pain. She *felt* helpless, but she was actually doing just what was necessary. What she needed from me was to be strong enough to *allow her to grieve*. What people in sorrow often need most is simply someone to be with them, to share the burden.

We, as therapists, friends, lovers, and family, too frequently interrupt the grief process because *we can't tolerate it ourselves*. Our own feelings of helplessness overwhelm us and make us rush in to smooth things over. But we shouldn't. Sometimes we are simply called upon to be in the pain, and wait.

I gave Marlene the following poem by T. S. Eliot, from "East Coker," in *Four Quartets*, which beautifully expresses the experience in the eye of the storm of despair:

> *I said to my soul, be still, and wait without hope*
> *For hope would be hope for the wrong thing; wait*
> *without love*
> *For love would be love of the wrong thing; there is*
> *yet faith*
> *But the faith and the love and the hope are all in*
> *the waiting.*
> *Wait without thought, for you are not ready for thought:*
> *So the darkness shall be the light, and the stillness*
> *the dancing.*

Getting through despair is like being in the ocean, caught up in the surf. The wave is too big to jump over—it catches you, throws you down under the surface and tosses you around. You can't see, can't hear, can't stand up. You're holding your breath, but time is running out and you feel as if your lungs will burst and you'll die before it's over. And then, suddenly, the water's calm, and you're free. You open your eyes and the whole world is there just as you left it, but it looks brighter and feels better as you gratefully breathe again, and sigh with relief.

The only way out of despair is through it, and Marlene made it through—she came out of the wave, out of the storm. Her tears washed away the pain, drop by drop, until the burden of her despair was lifted. By allowing me to go into the pain with her, Marlene discovered that her old belief was not true. People *can* help, and it's not necessary to do everything alone. She also found out that needing other people isn't shameful, it's human. From these realizations came new behaviors—she relaxed her defensive posture, softened, and became more accepting. Acquaintances deepened into friendships, and joy entered her life.

A year after finishing therapy, Marlene sent a card saying she had fallen in love. She wanted to share the excitement of her new relationship, and the hope that had replaced her despair. She thanked me for my help. I wrote back to Marlene, acknowledging her for having had the courage to reach out instead of giving up through suicide or resignation. And I reminded her that it was she who had done the emotional work that brought her to her new life. The seed of hope had been there all along, even when she didn't believe it. In the face of what appeared to her a hopeless condition, she chose to continue, to wait in the silence and wait out the pain.

CHAPTER 8

THERAPY IN RECOVERY FROM ADDICTIONS AND CODEPENDENCE

Everybody knows why addictions *don't* work, but what about why they *do*? Why are so many people compulsively repeating the same behaviors in spite of negative consequences? Do addictions serve some purpose? What are people looking for, that they will go to such extremes to find?

I believe the answer to these questions is twofold. First, and most obvious, people are trying to find pleasure and avoid pain. Drinking alcohol, smoking, eating, sex, spending money, and so on, are all fairly reliable, if questionable, ways to feel good and/or be distracted from discomfort or problems. They all can and do become extremely destructive, however, when taken to excess. It's natural to desire pleasurable experiences, and to need diversions from our difficulties at times. But when desire turns to compulsion, and escape becomes a desperate goal on a daily basis, recreation has become addiction. Almost any activity can become addictive, even something as healthy as exercising, or as natural as eating or making love. It is not the activity or substance itself that determines the addiction; rather, it's the person's *relationship* to that activity or substance. An addict is obsessed, thoughts race out of control, relentlessly centered around the object of desire; free will—the capacity to say no, or to be content without the object—is lost; the behavior is continued in spite of negative consequences to the person's life.

Generalizations cannot be made to distinguish recreation and dependence from addiction, because levels of tolerance vary, and each person's total makeup is unique. The amount of alcohol that constitutes alcoholism in one person may be considered only a dependence in another. It's not the quantity that is the determining factor; it's the way that quantity affects the person and impacts his or her life. However, the progression from recreation to addiction is more like a continuum, measured by a gradual increase in frequency and/or quantity of use, coinciding with a gradual decrease in self-control. What begins as a simple pleasure becomes an enslavement and a nightmare.

A saying from Alcoholics Anonymous describes the process succinctly:

First the man takes a drink
Then the drink takes a drink
Then the drink takes the man.

Addiction is very complex and as yet not thoroughly understood. Therefore, my attempt here is not to completely define it but to look at it in a slightly unorthodox manner. I believe the pursuit of pleasure and avoidance of pain are only superficial motivations of addiction, that on a deeper level *addicts are attempting to heal themselves without knowing what needs to be healed.* It is simultaneously a drive to get *out of* oneself and get *into* oneself—not only a movement away from pain, but also a movement, however misdirected, toward health. The addict is trying to soothe a hurting soul, express a suppressed feeling, right a past wrong, complete an incomplete self. The need to escape is rooted not so much in devil-may-care frivolity and recklessness as in an intolerably painful inner emotional world, and an inadequacy to cope with life.

John Bradshaw, in *Healing The Shame That Binds You*, writes:

> Neurotic shame is the fuel of all compulsive/addictive behaviors . . . the drivenness in any addiction is about the ruptured self, the belief that one is flawed as a person. The content of the addiction, whether it be an ingestive addiction or an activity addiction (like work, buying, or gambling) is an attempt at an intimate relationship.

I believe that the "intimate relationship" he names is a substitute for, or an attempt to find, a loving relationship with oneself. The "ruptured self" Bradshaw refers to is a result of childhood conditions that prevented a healthy self from developing, or damaged that self severely at some point along the way. People become addicts in the process of trying to feel whole instead of fragmented, connected to something instead of lost and alienated. They try to calm the torment of shame and anxiety and fill the void of inner emptiness. Speaking in spiritual terms, you might say that addictions reflect, and try to replace, a loss of connection to one's own soul.

Addicts pursuing bliss, peace, or wholeness bow in the service of their addictions. Objects of addiction become idols, exalted like false gods to be worshiped. Paradoxically, however, the ultimate *downfall* brought on by addiction potentially leads to rediscovery of the deeper self, or soul, and a true spiritual relationship. Recovery, when undertaken seriously and thoroughly, delivers addicts from slavery, giving them a new life, free from the addiction, and full of the richness of integrity, inner wholeness, and spiritual awakening.

To illustrate the process of recovery, let's use the example of Katie. When Katie came to see me, she was a compulsive overeater and binge spender. She weighed almost two hundred pounds, owed large sums of money on several credit cards, and felt out of control.

In the course of her therapy, I helped Katie clarify the feelings she experienced before, during, and after binges. Katie realized, "They're actually quite similar in a way—my two addictions. I start feeling lonely and sad, sometimes for no reason I can pinpoint, but other times because something has happened, like when my younger sister got married. I brood about my life and how empty it seems, like there's nothing good in it and there never will be. I worry because I don't have a husband and family of my own. The world seems to be turning without me. I'm on the sidelines looking in while everyone else is living. My mind goes around and around in circles until I feel scared and desperate. The next thing I know, I'm in the kitchen eating cookies, or I'm in a furniture store looking for a new dining room table."

Katie described her compulsive behavior very well; sometimes she made fun of herself, but mostly she was confused and discouraged about the trap she was in.

"Do you think about eating before you do it?" I asked her.

"Not really. Like I said, I just find myself in the kitchen, or in the bakery." She paused, "Well, actually there is a moment where the *idea* of eating or buying flashes in my head—I know it's what I want, and at the same time I know I shouldn't do it, and will regret it. But somehow the desire always wins out; there doesn't seem to be any real choice in the matter. It's like I'm possessed."

Katie, like every addict, was subject to the inner process of rationalization called *denial.* Overweight, in debt, and unhappy, she was able to effectively block out the truth of her situation, *reach for comfort from the very sources of her problems*, and thereby perpetuate her misery. In the clutches of denial, an addict is possessed. The ability to see or think clearly is lost, and true freedom is compromised. The soul has been delivered into addiction's greedy and consuming hands.

Why was Katie possessed? And what would it take to wrest back her soul? She was not being driven by a physical addiction as is true in alcoholism, which involves the body's acquired need for a substance. Her dependence was primarily emotional.

"What do you get when you eat or spend?" I asked. "Where do you go, emotionally?"

"I get full," she answered, without hesitating. "The emptiness goes away, and I get filled up. When I eat something sweet, I get filled up with sweetness. And when I buy things, I feel rich and luxurious. Like I can have anything I want. I feel free and sure of myself and happy and strong. And you should see my apartment—it's beautiful! I don't just buy *anything*, I buy beauty. I have good taste."

Katie's words were quite illuminating. Eating and spending weren't just diversions to distract her from loneliness and fear, they were vehicles to carry her to another emotional state altogether—a place where she could feel full instead of empty, secure instead of afraid, involved in life instead of left out of it. Furthermore, spending money on decorating was a means of creative expression for Katie, the only means she had. But why food, and why buying? Why those addictions and not others?

When we looked into Katie's childhood, the answer was readily evident. She had grown up in an affluent but emotionally deprived environment. Her parents were away from home most of the time on business trips or extended vacations. They left Katie with a live-in baby-sitter to whom they gave plenty of money, and instructions to buy Katie anything she wanted. When she cried, the baby-sitter fed her sweets, or lured her out of her tears with the promise of new presents. Without her parents around, Katie was lonely and anxious. The baby-sitter was quite passive and uninvolved, leaving Katie to play by herself. It was natural that she felt ostracized and set apart from life.

As an adult, Katie still carried the deep loneliness and estrangement of her childhood abandonment. When those feelings surfaced, her automatic response was to do the same thing her babysitter had done—to give herself food or presents. While in small doses these consolations could be comforting, in Katie's life they were excessive, compulsive, and devastating. Before therapy she was totally unaware of the pain inside her from the past. She knew only that her life was driven by an endless cycle of unhappiness, fear, craving, followed by binges of eating and spending, followed by remorse and shame, leading to more compulsive actions. She saw the sad irony of her addictions: While sweets helped her to feel full instead of empty and lonely, overeating actually contributed to her alienation, by adding pounds onto her body and deepening her self-hate. And, although buying things made her feel secure in the abundance of life, ultimately she was undermining her security by accumulating financial debt.

As Katie came to realize the source of her addictions, she came out of denial and decided to take action. For her, as for most people, willpower alone was not enough to break long-standing destructive patterns. I recommended the support and guidance of 12-Step self-help groups. Based on the model begun by Alcoholics Anonymous, 12-Step programs help thousands of people recover from all types of addictions. Katie joined Overeaters Anonymous and Debtors Anonymous.

I believe, for full recovery from addictions, both the compulsive behaviors and the emotional pain behind them must be dealt with. Often people come to therapy with hopes that as they understand themselves, their addictions will automatically cease. This is usually not true. Conversely, some people think, by stopping compulsive behavior through 12-Step programs, all their problems will be solved. Again this is not true. Addiction is a physical, emotional, mental, and spiritual problem. No doubt that ending a self-destructive pattern has a tremendously positive impact. However, without further emotional work, there is a higher risk of relapse and, very frequently, the substitution of a new addictive behavior to replace the old one.

When a compulsive behavior is finally eliminated, the addict's inner world is shaken—a void is created, feelings begin to surface, and psychic disorder reigns. At this point, a person without sufficient help may shut down emotionally, as the only method of coping. Addictions, as I said, function both to soothe and to attempt to connect people to something they need in life. A person who is determined not to relapse may become emotionally rigid, to defend against the experience of living sober—an experience which at first feels far too painful and chaotic. This rigid way of living is referred to in A.A. as "white knuckle sobriety" or being "dry" but not sober. The alcohol is gone, but the alcoholic behavior remains. Quitting just isn't enough.

In his book *Stage II Recovery*, Earnie Larsen says:

> Abstinence may get you out of a bad place, but getting you out of a bad place just gets you out; it is not the same as getting to a good one.
>
> Abstinence and the ability to have a happy life are not the same thing. As one man said, "Abstinence is like standing up at the starting line. The race hasn't started yet, but at least you are standing up rather than lying down."

Through her involvement with O.A. and D.A., Katie began to change. As she pulled in the reins on her overeating and spending, she was confronted with the feelings and pain she had been avoiding for so long. She could no longer binge her way into the delusion that everything was fine. She was forced to face the truth and work through her fears. In addition, her customary creative outlet was now blocked, requiring a reevaluation of the place of creativity in her life.

In *Witness to the Fire*, Linda Leonard talks about recovery itself as a creative process:

> What is true of the artist struggling to create a painting or a poem is true of the addict struggling to create a new being. The act of creation requires fighting the battle and knowing the battleground. Addicts who survive the deadly battle with addiction go through a process similar to the creative process. . . . The courage the addict must have to change is similar to the courage it takes to create. The art of creation requires a leap into the unknown. To create means to "bring into being." This is tantamount to bringing something out of "nothing."

Katie was determined and courageous. She worked hard to curtail her compulsivity, attended meetings regularly, doing what the 12-Step programs recommended. She remained open to her feelings in therapy and did not shut down. We discussed her strong creative drive which had never really been tapped. Now that she couldn't shop and decorate, that drive was frustrated.

"What can I do about it?" she asked. "The only alternative I've come up with is clothing. Now that I'm losing weight I have to buy new clothes, and I get a lot of enjoyment choosing styles and colors. But that's still shopping! It's too easy for me to get compulsive about it."

I asked Katie to think back to her childhood and those long hours at home with her baby-sitter. What did she do? Had she gravitated toward any art form at that time?

"Well, yes," she answered eagerly. "I used to love music—I'd bang on pots and pans, and sing. Someone bought me a tiny, toy piano, too." Suddenly her face saddened. "I never knew how to use it though, so I'd just play with it for a few minutes and then give up." She brightened again. "I was better at painting—that was fun. At school we always had paints and easels, and I spent hours watching the colors." Katie looked pensive as memories drifted through her mind.

"Sounds like you have two directions there," I said.

"I guess so," she said softly. "Funny but I had forgotten all about them. I must have been born creative! I never thought of myself that way. When I was little, I wanted to grow up to be a musician or a painter, that's what I told myself. I *must* have some talent if I had such a strong interest, don't you think?"

"Probably. How did that interest disappear?"

She looked sad again. "I don't know. Nobody noticed. Nobody talked to me about it or gave me any guidance. Some of my friends at school took music lessons but I didn't. I guess my parents were just too busy to see who I was and help me develop my talents. That really makes me feel awful. Actually, they probably wouldn't have encouraged me, even if they had seen. They were so money oriented, they would definitely have thought of any art as unsuitable for my career—too flighty, too unpredictable, too out-of-the-mainstream. They wouldn't have helped."

Katie realized she was on her own. It was up to her to bring out and nurture her latent creativity. For most of her life, eating had taken the place of love, and decorating her apartment had taken the place of music and painting. She finally had the opportunity to make more meaningful choices for her future.

The story of Katie is simple in its clarity. Her addictions dulled pain and served as *substitutes* for what she really needed. But what happens when addictions appear to *give* people what they really need? It's confusing when chemicals or compulsive activities seem to serve a positive purpose.

Richard and Leila were acquaintances of mine years ago. We used to see one another occasionally at small parties. People always remarked on how different they were from each other—Leila was boisterous and outgoing, Richard was quiet and withdrawn. By the end of an evening, however, Richard had become outgoing too, with the aid of a few drinks.

Leila confided in me during one of those evenings: "Richard is so difficult. Most of the time he's quiet and sweet, which I like, but it's too extreme. I never know how he feels about anything. Then we come to these parties, he drinks and totally changes. When we go home he's all over me, wanting to go to bed, telling me how much he loves me. The only time he tells me he loves me is when he's had a few. Or, he might be in a rage and start fighting with me the minute we hit the front door. He never yells at me except when he's drunk."

These reactions to alcohol confused Leila. Richard was an alcoholic, but he didn't drink every day, so his problem wasn't easy to recognize. Alcohol was the key he used to unlock feelings that were otherwise suppressed. I talked to Leila about addiction, A.A., Al-Anon, and therapy. (Al-Anon is the self-help group for anyone closely involved with an alcoholic.)

Leila's reaction was mixed. "Well, of course I know he's got some kind of a problem, but to tell you the truth I'm not so sure I *want* him to stop drinking. Even though he gets out of control when he's drunk, at least he's *fun*! I'd hate it if I never heard him tell me he loved me anymore. And if he never fought with me, he'd walk around with that pinched frown he gets on his face when he's mad and won't admit it." Leila was about to walk away from me. She thought she had to choose between a drunk man who could love her passionately, or a sober man who couldn't.

I tried to reassure her that there was a third alternative: "Alcohol gets rid of whatever fears he has about expressing himself. So quitting drinking would only solve half of the problem. He'd stop being so erratic and extreme, but he'd be permanently shut down. Of course you wouldn't want that. But therapy could help him uncover and work through those fears so he would have the freedom to express himself even better, and be sober too. He wouldn't have to walk around with a pinched face."

Many people drink to be able to release feelings. In sobriety, the recovering person must learn to work through and express feelings *without* alcohol. That task *must* be accomplished, or the risk of relapse is much higher.

Most people have to first address their compulsive behavior before they can do the deeper work of emotional healing. The willingness to give up an addiction doesn't come easily. Addicts generally try every way they can to get around this decision. An image that well illustrates the avoidance process is that of a brick wall, miles high, miles deep in the ground, and extending indefinitely to the right and to the left. The addict tries to go over, under and around the wall, but can never succeed, and wastes years trying. Finally comes the realization that the only way out is to confront it head-on, and break through. Once the decision is made, withdrawal begins; it's a painful and trying time.

Dr. Gerald May puts it this way, in *Addiction and Grace*:

> Any authentic struggle with [addiction] must involve deprivation. We have to go hungry and unsatisfied; we have to ache for something. . . . Withdrawal symptoms are real, and one way or another, they will be experienced. If we can both accept and *expect* this pain, we will be much better prepared to face struggles with specific attachments. We might even come to see it as birth pain, heralding the process of our delivery from slavery to freedom.

Some people need to be in therapy for a while, before they're able to face withdrawal. Therapy provides personal support and understanding to buffer the intense shame addicts feel. *Knowing there are reasons for addictions helps people to see their behaviors as reflections of internal pain (and, in the case of alcoholism, a physical illness), rather than evidence of being weak, bad, or immoral.* The relationship with a therapist provides a new type of structure, a new form of connection and intimacy which acts as a counterbalance to the addiction. The therapy room is a home for the budding healthy self which begins merely as an idea or a hope. In time, the healthy part grows until it eclipses the previously dominant, addictive self. Nevertheless, as difficult as withdrawal is, accomplishing it is only half the battle.

Often after a dependency upon alcohol, drugs, or other substances is overcome, what's revealed is codependency or relationship addiction. Codependence and relationship addiction are similar and share some common behaviors, and both are too complex to be fully defined here. Codependence refers most often to an attachment to one person, excessive care-taking or "rescuing," and a subjugation or denial of one's own feelings, needs, and wants in order to preserve a relationship. A relationship addict may exhibit codependent behaviors, but may also be involved with more than one person, and may be more concerned with *being* rescued than with rescuing. The relationship addict gets "high" through the other person. Both involve denial, obsession, loss of control, and avoidance of internal problems. Both derive the temporary illusion of meaning and self-esteem through involvement in someone else's life.

There's a saying, "Addicts don't have relationships, they take hostages." This saying reflects the deep need of the addict for help, the self's misguided attempt to strengthen itself through attachment. If underlying all addictions is the unhealed self wounded by childhood relationships, it is no wonder that an addict's love relationships in adulthood would be adversely affected. "People addictions" clearly and poignantly demonstrate the emotional problems underlying compulsivity. Because of childhood abuse or deprivation, the relationship addict lacks internal security and self-love, and longs to possess and control someone else who embodies those essential characteristics. Unfortunately for the addict, the person sought after often does not feel inclined to be "taken hostage," and pulls away, thus creating a pursuer/distancer dynamic. The addict is attracted to people who appear to have something he or she needs; the "magical quality" sought could be almost anything, and is usually determined by the addict's personal history. For example, the essential ingredient could be strength, if the addict feels weak, or it could be beauty, if the addict feels unattractive. Often the quality sought was present in one or both parents, and the attachment to that quality is an attempt (unconsciously) to resolve something from the past. Other examples are self-confidence, intelligence, youth, maturity, spirituality, spontaneity, sexuality, creativity, independence, power, stability, self-control, humor, athletic ability, adventurousness. However, the attempt to acquire any characteristic through attachment to another person is doomed to failure.

Let's look at the story of Angela, to illustrate. When Angela first came to my office, she was depressed, ashamed, and confused. Her six-year involvement with a man named Rafael had slowly drained her energy, her confidence, and her health.

She told me this story: "When I met Rafael, I was only twenty-two and he was thirty-four. From the first minute I saw him, I was crazy about him. He's Italian, tall, dark curly hair, intense eyes, incredibly handsome, and exciting. On our first date, he took me on his yacht with all his super-powerful, rich friends, and as I watched him looking out over the ocean, I thought I'd die of happiness. We drank champagne all day and I ended up sleeping there on the boat with him. I hadn't intended to, actually, but by evening I was pretty drunk, and he was very persuasive, so I did it. The next morning he suggested I stay the weekend, and it was heaven. I thought my life had finally begun.

"Well, after the weekend, I went home and didn't hear from him for three weeks. At first I was flying so high, it didn't bother me, but little by little my fantasy crumbled and was replaced by fear, hurt, and shame. Where was he? Did I do something that weekend to alienate him? What did I do? How could he have been so loving and then disappear? My mind raced in total obsession, all day and all night. I couldn't sleep or eat. All of a sudden, he called! He talked to me so seductive and charming, just like before, and invited me on a weekend sail to a nearby island. Well of course I jumped at the chance. I was so relieved to hear from him, I never even ventured to mention the three weeks in between.

"It's been that way now for six years. We'll spend the most incredible time together and then I won't hear from him for weeks. After the first couple of go-rounds I began to speak up. He always made light of it like it was no big deal. 'Oh, honey, I've just been so busy,' he'd say, or, 'I had so many visitors this month from Italy, I just forgot to call you. But I meant to call, I was thinking of you.' Slowly I got more desperate and upset and began to question him about other women. 'Oh no, never,' he'd answer. 'I'm not like that; I'm not the stereotype.' Eventually I got angry and tried to force the issue. 'Tell me what's wrong!' I'd yell. 'Why do you treat me this way? You don't really love me. Just admit it and let me go!' 'But I *do* love you,' he said. 'But I hate these conflicts; I don't want to hurt you, so maybe we should stop seeing each other.'

"Well, that's all I needed to hear to shut me up for the next several months. The thought of losing him was unbearable."

"What is so precious to you about him?" I asked.

"Everything!" she wailed. "His life! He's got it all—he's gorgeous, super-sexy, rich, independent, and even artistic. With him I'm in ecstasy."

"But it's only part-time ecstasy," I said.

"Right." She looked perplexed and despairing. "I've tried and tried to adjust to the situation but I can't. I can't leave either, and he will not change. Now it's gotten more complicated. He introduced me to cocaine, and at first I just had a little when he gave it to me. Now I've started buying my own. I use it whenever I get too down or when I know I'm going to see him, to be sure I'm 'up' enough. And what's worse, these separation periods leave me so devastated that I can't sleep, and instead of lying awake all night worrying, I take Valium. I know my health is being affected—I feel tired and edgy and my face looks worn out."

Angela was addicted to Rafael. When she was with him she got a "fix." It made her feel excited, loved, and invulnerable. Apart from him, she went into withdrawal—feeling abandoned, miserable, confused, and manipulated. Why couldn't she leave? A woman who was looking for a truly intimate, lasting relationship would probably not have been as attracted to Rafael as Angela had been, and would probably not have spent the night with him right away. Or, if she had fallen in love with him, a healthier woman would have said, "I love him, he's romantic and thrilling, but I can't trust what he says, and can't count on him at all, so I have to let it go." A woman whose self-esteem was higher would have seen Rafael for the player he was. If she wanted more than a part-time playmate, she would have gotten out. Instead, Angela kept doubting her own intuition and tried to make truth out of Rafael's lies and excuses. She tried to *understand* him: "But he *does* have a big family and a lot of work to do. He really is busy, so why can't I just accept it?" Or, she questioned her own worth and lovableness: "Maybe I'm just not totally his type. He likes me because I'm blond and American, but he's torn between his culture and mine. I try to be what I think he wants—a perfect woman—but I'm not even sure what that is!"

I could see how far down Angela's addiction had taken her. Trying to win Rafael's commitment and love, she was losing herself. She was unraveling emotionally after years of strain, disappointment, and struggle. Now drugs were contributing to her downward spiral.

She cried bitterly, saying: "No one understands me. Even my

friends are sick of me. They think I'm either stupid or a masochist! I'm not! I don't like pain, I really don't!"

I did understand Angela, and told her so. I knew she didn't like pain but was powerless to stop herself. We started working together and I recommended she attend one of the 12-Step programs (like Co-Dependents Anonymous or Sex and Love Addicts Anonymous) which focus on breaking patterns of addiction to a person.

As we delved into Angela's past the sources of her behavior were readily apparent: "My parents got divorced when I was really young, because my father was always running around with other women, and my mother just got sick of it. He was a musician and had this wild life where he stayed up late at night and slept all day, and half the time he was away doing out-of-town gigs. He'd take me to the clubs during rehearsals and let me sit up on a table close to the stage. I just thought he was everything. But I didn't get to see him much. Most of the time I was stuck at home with my brothers."

"Where was your mother?" I asked.

"Well, they never had any money, of course, so usually she was out working at some crummy job, and when she'd come home, she'd just sit in front of the television. I had to do most of the cooking and cleaning for everyone."

The script for Angela's relationship with Rafael was written in her childhood. In the darkness of her mother's emotional absence, and the burden of her domestic responsibilities, the only joy was her father's occasional attention. He was her link to the world, to love, to fun, and to freedom. She worshiped him. When he wasn't around, she waited for him.

"As a child I used to write letters to him, but we never knew where he was. So I'd put some made-up address on the envelope and mail it anyway, and then pretend that he got it. I always wished he loved us more so he'd come around more often. Every day I'd look out and wonder if he was going to show up."

The sparse and inconsistent attention Angela was given as a child deprived her of inner security. She never developed a sense of certainty that she was loved and lovable, and that she could count on others to be there for her. She was given no connection to the world, no support in becoming an independent adult with direction and creative goals. Therefore, her adult life was unplanned, unorganized, and unfulfilling. She was depressed and unable to find ways to succeed in life. She felt impotent, lost, and alone.

When Rafael came along, doors seemed to open; she suddenly felt alive, attractive, and energized. Life was exciting, and through Raphael, she could participate in it. Just like her father, Rafael was Angela's ticket to paradise—temporarily. He took her out of emptiness and self-doubt, and brought her into his world of people and passion, making her feel loved and special. Rafael's sailing was the equivalent of her father's music—a link to the creative, spiritual dimension. Both Rafael and Angela's father lived creatively and passionately, expressing qualities that Angela possessed, but never developed; Angela had a strong attraction to nature, to art, and to metaphysics but, because of insecurity, she rarely pursued those longings.

In order to free herself from addiction, Angela had to go through a transformation. First, she had to admit the truth about her relationship with Rafael, and stop seeing him. He was never going to be more than a temporary escape, followed by devastating abandonment. Second, she had to go through withdrawal, allowing herself to feel the pain and grieve the loss. Third, she also had to face and process feelings about her childhood.

Admitting the truth about Rafael led to sadness and rage about her father—yes, he was her ticket to paradise, but he also failed her through his self-centered absorption in his own life. He had given her very little of his time, and no way to depend upon him, no addresses when he was gone, no phone calls, and no dates of return. The pain she suffered as a child had been intense. Her father's actions (combined with her mother's lack of attention) had set up Angela to view herself as a helpless victim, and view men as all-powerful gods.

Through therapy and the 12 Steps, Angela did let go of Rafael. By working through the pain of the past, her inner self began to heal and strengthen. She understood that the abandonment she endured was not her fault, and did not mean she was unlovable. Slowly she developed the confidence and self-worth to ask herself what she really needed and wanted.

Finally, Angela was able to believe she could hope for more than sparse and inconsistent love. She began to evaluate her interests and formulate goals, realizing that in order to avoid repeating the patterns of addiction to men, she had to develop her own powers and her own passions. If she wanted an adventurous and exciting life, she had to create it herself. Much was required of her, but she rose to the challenge. For Angela, as for many other addicts, the path out of addiction would be more than a relief from a downward spiral of misery, more than simply a return to the person she was before she met Rafael. For Angela, recovery took her out of slavery into freedom, emotional growth, creativity, and a spiritual awareness she never had. Not all addicts embrace their recovery as Angela did—but those who do, receive more than they ever imagined.

From Linda Leonard's *Witness to the Fire*:

> Out of the wounds of addiction, consciously and courageously faced, can come creativity and healing. This is the call that challenges the recovering addict—the call to creativity. It is a call that requires courage—transforming one's addictive afflictions to creativity. Whether one creates a new spiritual self, an act of love that opens up the possibility of recovery and transformation to another, or a work of art per se, it generously gives back the life it has received.

CHAPTER 9

THE HEALING RELATIONSHIP

Steven talked, during a therapy session with me, about his mistrust of people and his reasons for avoiding emotional intimacy.

I asked, "Do you think that attitude enters into our relationship as well?"

He looked shocked. "Our *relationship*? What do you mean? I don't think of this as a relationship!"

Steven's reaction to my question was a common one. Most people see the association between therapist and client as either a business transaction where a service is provided for a fee, or a doctor-patient interaction in which a problem will be identified and a cure given. In fact, a unique relationship *does* develop between therapist and client, one that differs from both business and medicine. This chapter is about that relationship and the part it plays in bringing about change.

The healing process of therapy occurs on several levels simultaneously: First, as I've already stressed, is the very important accessing of memories and feelings from the past, and the expression of them to someone who understands and cares. Second is the linking of past occurrences to present-day situations, revealing re-creations of unconscious patterns, which can then be more readily changed. The third level is the *actual experiencing* of those unconscious patterns *within* the interaction between therapist and client.

Until conditioned beliefs, patterns, and attitudes are brought to our attention, we're unaware of them. We enter situations *expecting* people to behave, and events to occur, in certain ways; if they don't, we may not believe what we see—our preconceptions distort the truth. The therapist clarifies those inaccurate beliefs and attitudes. Ironically, the client brings the same preconceptions to the therapeutic relationship, entering therapy with certain expectations of the therapist, and reacting in ways that reflect beliefs learned in childhood. The therapist, however, understands this dynamic, and interprets the interactions *in the moment*, bringing patterns to the client's awareness in a powerful way.

To illustrate, let's go back to Steven and his fear of getting close to people. When I asked about his parents, he said, "I was a pretty intense kid, I guess. My father was always yelling at me to calm down, sit down, stop running around, and stop making so much noise. I'd slow down for a few minutes but then start up again. It was just too hard to be still."

"That's pretty normal for kids," I said.

"Yeah, well maybe so, but not in my house. Sometimes I'd get really frustrated and start yelling back at my dad. Then he'd come after me and it was all over." Steven's face showed his rage and pain.

"What do you mean 'it was all over'?" I asked.

"He'd start slapping me, and keep on going until he beat me down to the ground." Steven struggled not to cry. He was determined to keep talking, and went on. "My mother would rush over and try to stop him, but he'd shove her out of the way. She'd just stand there crying or run out of the room."

Naturally Steven didn't trust people. Why should he? His own parents had taught him to be afraid to show his feelings. Exuberance was met with anger. When he protested, he was beaten by his father and abandoned by his ineffectual mother.

I went back to my question about his fears entering into our relationship. "Well, based on what you've told me, I imagine you'd be afraid to show your feelings to me, too."

Steven looked astonished. "Well, I suppose I am. Maybe up to a point I could trust you, but not beyond."

"Where's that point?" I asked. "And what would happen if you passed it?"

"Who knows? Maybe if I got too rowdy in here or too loud or aggressive, you'd tell me to leave. You'd say you couldn't work with me. Or maybe if I got mad at you, I'd hurt your feelings. I wouldn't want to do that."

Steven's fears reflected his experiences as a child. He was afraid I wouldn't—or couldn't—tolerate his feelings, that I would punish him like his father did, or crumble like his mother. It's very common for clients to fear they are too much for their therapist. Clients have expressed fears to me of being too needy, too scared, too angry, too sad. They're afraid I won't be strong enough for them, just as their parents weren't. It's usually very touching for both of us when a client finds out I *can* be strong enough, and they are not "too much" this time. These moments also bring out grief, shame, and rage, as they realize what they missed in the past.

We transfer feelings from our past onto people in our present lives; it happens all the time. The advantage in the therapeutic relationship is that the *transference* can be observed, analyzed, and used for the purpose of healing.

Michael Kahn, in his book *Between Therapist and Client*, writes about one of the crucial reasons why the therapeutic relationship differs from others, and, as such, is useful to the client:

> Beginning with our parents, we encounter people throughout our lives who have so much to defend that we learn, at worst, to keep our feelings to ourselves or, at best, to expect the expression of those feelings to be met with little more than a defensive riposte. . . . The therapeutic relationship is crucially different in that expressed feelings about the therapist are not met with a defensive countermove, but rather with warm encouragement to explore them further.

I would insert the word *hopefully* in his quote: ". . . *hopefully* not met with a defensive countermove." If a therapist is not skillful, or is inattentive to the nuances of the relationship, or is overwhelmed by his or her own unconscious emotions, defensiveness is quite likely.

Kahn is aware of the danger inherent in a therapist's insensitive reactions. He goes on to say, "Much that transpires between therapist and client is subtle indeed. . . . Until one has grasped just how subtle and complex the relationship can be, and how important the therapist becomes to the client, one is likely to seriously underestimate how easy it is to damage the therapy. . . . An offhand remark or thoughtless joke can cause pain or confusion the client may not be able to acknowledge."

I encountered defensive therapists several times during my own journey as a client, and I remember well how painful it was. Luckily, since I was studying psychology, I knew enough to challenge their defensiveness and, if my protest was met with further defense, I knew enough to seek help elsewhere.

Therapists who cannot recognize and acknowledge their own reactions, but instead fight to win against their clients, are doing a great disservice. A client is vulnerable and looking to the therapist as an authority. Hearing defensive arguments can easily cause a client to feel wrong and ashamed. This type of interaction only serves to replay the same invalidation of feelings the client has always experienced.

On the other hand, I, as a therapist, being human too, have also been conditioned by childhood experiences. Just as in any other relationship, I'm going to have my own reactions—called *countertransference*—to a client's feelings about me. However, unlike other relationships in my personal life, as a therapist I am present for the purpose of helping my client; I do my best to process my feelings internally, or with a colleague, and express them to the client in nondefensive ways and at the times I consider appropriate.

Therapists vary on the extent they focus on, and explore, their relationship with clients as an aspect of their work. When psychoanalysis began as part of the medical profession, analysts viewed the transference as very important, although they attempted to remain neutral, disclosing little, if anything, about themselves. They spoke infrequently during sessions, occasionally offering interpretations. From that, we derived the stereotype of the aloof, unfeeling psychiatrist. Actually, the silence did not mean lack of feeling; it was believed to be a means of evoking more from the client's unconscious. Therapists today range from the traditional, to a more casual self-revealing style. Some therapists focus strongly on their relationship with clients, others not at all.

In my practice, I value the relationship with my clients as a rich source of information as well as an avenue of healing. How much we focus on the relationship, and how much I choose to reveal about myself, depends upon the needs of each individual. The nuances are quite complex and worthy of careful evaluation.

In Steven's case, working on our relationship proved to be extremely important. In later sessions, we discovered that his fear of being "too much" held him back in many ways.

He said, "I guess I see you as an authority figure. To be honest, I hate authority figures. I feel meek, as if I have to be on my best behavior all the time. At work, I walk around like I'm invisible or something. I've had some great ideas which could maybe get me promoted, but I'm afraid to show them to anybody."

Learning to express his full potential was the challenge for Steven. By working through his fears *of me*, he was able to process the blocks to self-expression formed in childhood. Steven needed to hear my encouragement of his anger toward authority. He did not need to hear anything about me personally.

Once he said, "It's weird, in a way, talking about my problems and not knowing anything about you. But, actually, I don't *want* to know about your life. If I knew what bothered you, I probably wouldn't be able to keep on expressing my feelings. I'd be afraid to hurt you or burden you. I'd feel like taking care of you."

Steven was seeing me the way he saw his mother. If *I* had problems, he thought, they would overwhelm me and make me unable to care for him. He'd have to care for me instead.

Many fears hover in the minds of clients—fears about what I might think of them, feel toward them, or do to them. If I don't bring out those fears, sensitively, they remain unspoken, blocking our progress.

Another man, Bill, brought out a concern often expressed. After we had worked together for a while, I observed that he rarely let himself be vulnerable in front of me and, when I encouraged going deeper into feelings, he snapped at me with a sarcastic remark.

Given the opportunity, Bill got honest about something that had held him back, "You *say* you want to hear all this stuff about me. But why should I talk? You don't *really* care about me. You only listen because I *pay* you. You're probably bored to death hearing the same stuff over and over, day in and day out."

"So you think I'm not interested in what you have to say?" I asked.

"You got it," he answered sullenly.

"That must feel awful to you," I went on. "Coming here for help and thinking I'm bored."

"Don't give me that 'I understand how you feel' crap. Everything you say is just a manipulation to get me to open up. It's all part of your job. You're just a manipulator."

This moment with Bill, and moments like them, are difficult. He was afraid to trust me, and anything I said merely added to his mistrust and despair.

I stepped out of my role for a moment, to approach him more personally. "Bill," I said, "it's true you pay me to listen to you. It's true that it's my job. But money can't buy caring, and I do care about you. If all I wanted was money, I would have chosen a different career. I really do want to help you."

His expression softened a little.

I continued, "It sounds to me like no one has ever really been interested in what you feel. If no one has cared about you before, of course it would be hard to believe that I would care about you now, especially since you pay me."

Tears of emotion filled his eyes. He was silent for a while and then said, "You're right, I guess. I'm afraid to believe you care. I think you're just stringing me along for the money, and then you forget about me the minute I walk out of here. People have always used me. My parents made me work for them since I was seven; both my wives had a constant list of things for me to do. No one ever asked me how I felt about anything. I think people are just looking out for themselves."

Bill had never shared his pain with anyone. To do so now was going to require a risk, and the willingness to believe in something not experienced before—that another person wanted to help him. Also required of Bill was to acknowledge the truth of his past, and to work through the feelings of what had happened to him.

He had to rise above his fears long enough to enter into the therapeutic relationship. He had to be brave enough to not use those fears as an excuse to go back into emotional hiding.

People who have been forced by circumstances to become emotionally closed and independent struggle hard in therapy against internal resistance. On the one hand, they want to let down their guard and lean on someone; on the other hand, their lifelong instincts are telling them not to do it.

Another person caught in this bind was Caroline. After some deep work and rewarding emotional growth, she expressed gratitude to me for helping her, saying, "It really means a lot having you in my life. I don't know what I'd do without you." At the end of the session, she said, "See you next week."

But, in a couple of days, I received a card in the mail from Caroline:

> *Dear Joyce,*
> *Thanks again for all your kindness. You have helped me so much. I've decided to quit therapy for a while. Just wanted to let you know.*
>
> *Sincerely,*
> *Caroline*

Considering the contrast between our last session and the message on the card, and considering what I knew about Caroline, I guessed what was happening. I called her and proposed we meet to talk about this sudden decision. She agreed.

In my office again, Caroline looked distressed and confused. When I asked what prompted her change of heart, she looked even more uncomfortable and answered, evasively, "Well, I don't know exactly. I just figured it would be better to quit now. I can't keep coming here forever, you know."

Her last sentence confirmed my belief, so I asked gently, "Are you worried about getting stuck here? Becoming too dependent on me?"

"Yes," she answered, eyes downcast in embarrassment. "You're already too important to me, and I'm not important to you at all."

This led us into an exploration of Caroline's feelings of self-worth. Her well-being and healing were important to me, but she didn't believe it, because my importance to her loomed so large. At this point in her life she had few friends and no family to support her. Her parents had been addicted to drugs throughout her childhood, and were still addicted. Even though her mother and father had always been around the house, they were so preoccupied with buying, selling, and using drugs that their attention to Caroline was superficial at best. Of course she felt unimportant to her parents; getting high was their number one priority. She definitely came second. Emotionally, they were never fully present.

Processing the sadness of emotional abandonment was painful for Caroline. It was frightening for her to feel the impact of her aloneness. But she was able to separate her fears of being unimportant to her parents from her fears of being unimportant to me. She decided to continue therapy and allow herself to stay vulnerable with me.

However, it wasn't long before another layer of feelings surfaced—anger. She burst into a flood of words at the beginning of one session.

"You keep telling me it's okay for me to need you. That's easy for you to say. What good are you to me if I can only see you one or two hours a week? What if I need you more than that? What if I need you all the time? Too bad for me, that's what. Why should I even get started when it'll never be enough? It would be worse to let myself need you and then have you disappoint me. I'd rather just stay the way I am—even if I'm lonely, at least I can count on myself."

Caroline was expressing a very poignant feeling, one shared by many people in therapy when they allow themselves to open up emotionally. The vast, unmet needs from early childhood deprivation seem to all rush in when finally given an opportunity after so many years. The need appears so immense that patients think nothing short of constant attention could fill it. In fact, constant attention *is* what very young children do require, and deserve. People who were deprived of attention and had to fend for themselves are overwhelmed, momentarily, by the force of their own needs.

"You're right," I said to Caroline. "I can't be with you all the time. And I understand that the time we have isn't enough."

"No it isn't!" she cried. She was enraged at me, and hurt, too.

We spent many sessions working on this aspect of our relationship. The angry, abandoned child in Caroline wanted to punish me for hurting her, for being unavailable, just like her parents. She vacillated between self-righteous anger and self-effacing pain. The flip side of her anger was the shame that deprived and abused children feel, the shame that asks, "What did I do? Why don't you love me? What's wrong with me? Am I so bad? What can I do to make you love me and stay with me?"

By empathizing with Caroline, and helping her work through her grief, I actually *was* being available to her. Of course I could never undo the damage her parents had done, even if I stayed with her twenty-four hours a day. But, the *reexperiencing* of previously suppressed feelings *in the present*, within the relatively safe context of our relationship, afforded her a valuable chance for healing. Unlike her parents, I was *emotionally* present—willing to listen, understand, and care.

In *Between Therapist and Client*, Michael Kahn, addressing his views of the therapeutic relationship, has this to say specifically about reexperiencing past feelings:

> A reexperiencing therapist believes that the client must have an opportunity to relive emotionally the impulses,

> the anxieties, and the conflicts of his past and to relive them under certain specified conditions. . . . While it is necessary for clients eventually to understand the roots of their difficulties, that understanding cannot be delivered as an explanation. It must emerge from the clients' reexperiencing certain aspects of their past. And this reexperiencing must occur within the therapeutic relationship.

Many people who come to therapy are like Steven, Bill, and Caroline. They have lived in emotional isolation, unable to trust or need others. In therapy, they work to change that pattern. Some people, however, are just the opposite—through their life circumstances, they have become *too* accustomed to leaning on others, and must work toward greater independence.

Evelyn's story is a good example. When she called me on the phone for a first appointment, she was soft-spoken and almost ingratiating in her tone. An eager client, she quickly moved into a vulnerable, open manner in her sessions. She had no trouble telling me every detail of her most private activities, and seemed to hang on my every word, often asking my advice. Her eyes appeared innocent—generally she seemed younger and less mature than her age of twenty-nine. She cried easily and didn't show embarrassment about it. What brought her to therapy was a problem experienced by many young women: she was locked in a conflict between starting a family or pursuing her career. Initially, her anguish seemed to reflect a real ambivalence inside her. But as we continued to work together, more was revealed. The "have children or start a career" issue was only a smokescreen for a deeper struggle Evelyn was unaware of, a struggle for her independence. My discovery of this deeper issue came when I asked Evelyn to tell me about her relationship with her parents.

She said, "Oh they're great! We've always been a very close family. As a matter of fact I'm going to see them tonight—I have dinner with them three or four nights a week. I tell my mother *everything*. There's nothing about me she doesn't know. We've been talking a lot about my decision lately."

"And what do they say?" I asked.

"They *definitely* want me to marry my boyfriend, Frank. They like him. And they think we should have children right away, not waste any more time. My father says women are getting too much like men these days, and should be better mothers instead of wearing business suits and running after money. Mom says I shouldn't let go of Frank because he's a good man and I'm almost thirty and haven't been married yet. And she says it gets harder to have kids, the older you get."

Evelyn's forehead was all scrunched up with worry. I asked what she thought of her parents' opinions.

"Well, I guess they're right. I mean, maybe they're right—oh, I don't know, I'm so confused! That's why I'm here. What do *you* think?" She looked desperate, putting her head in her hands.

It was clear that Evelyn was strongly influenced by her family, so much that she had difficulty knowing her own mind. When I questioned her further about the family, she told me many stories, all with a common theme: Since childhood, all major decisions of Evelyn's life were made *for* her by her parents. They steered her, step by step, in the directions they wanted her to go. Although their involvement was done in the name of love, and (in their own minds at least) with Evelyn's best interests at heart, they effectively robbed her of the freedom to make decisions. Their own fears, and consequent need to control, prevented Evelyn from developing the ability to take independent action. She simply didn't know her own mind, and didn't trust her intuition.

I commented on my observations, saying, "It sounds like your parents have had a lot to do with the choices you've made. Have you ever decided anything important on your own?"

Evelyn's face flushed with shame. She was silent for a few minutes and then said quietly, "Not much. Is that bad? I figure they're older than I am, so they probably know better. That's what they tell me anyway."

"What do you think it would be like for you to make a decision by yourself?" I asked.

"I don't know," she answered.

"Well, let's go back to the decision about Frank. Do you have an idea of which way you'd really like to go?"

After a pause, she said, "To tell you the truth, I don't see what the big rush is to have children. Who says just because you're a woman you have to have children anyway? I don't even know if I'd be a good mother. What if I *never* had any children?"

"A lot of women make that decision," I said.

"I know, but my parents would never forgive me; they'd never understand. That's why I have to hide . . ." Her voice trailed off and she looked frightened and hesitant.

"Hide?"

"Hide from them," she said resolutely. It was obvious she had made up her mind to talk more openly to me now. "I might as well tell you the truth, if I want you to help me. Frank, my so-called boyfriend, is really just a friend who helps me out by pretending to be my boyfriend once in a while, around my parents. My real lover is a woman, Patricia. I feel like it's all gotten out of hand now, though, with my parents pushing me to get married and have children. I don't know what to do. I can't see my way out."

"What if you told them the real situation?" I asked.

"Ha! What a joke. They'd disown me. Or kill me."

"So you're maintaining a false front for their acceptance. But what is it costing you?"

"What do you mean?"

"Well, your secrecy and the cover-up must be very stressful. You can't be real around your family," I said.

She looked sad and a little lost, saying "You're right." Evelyn felt stuck between two unsatisfying options—to please herself and lose her parents, or to please her parents and lose herself.

As we continued to work on this struggle, more feelings surfaced. I asked again what it would be like for her to make an independent decision, even if it was in disagreement with her parents.

"Scary," she said. "Very scary. I feel like I'd be doing something so wrong to go against them. And maybe my decision would be a mistake and then I'd be out there all alone, with no one on my side anymore." Suddenly she shifted. "You still haven't told me what *you* think I should do," she insisted. "That's what I'm here for, so you can help me."

I was silent for a long time, and Evelyn began to look even more uncomfortable. I didn't rush in with a response, because I saw how she was, unknowingly, looking to me to make a decision *for* her just as her parents always did. And, I also knew that if I gave advice that didn't fit her true desires, she would rebel against it, or follow it and then resent my advice and hate herself for having followed it. The answer for Evelyn was not in finding the right advice—it was in developing the self-confidence and strength to follow her own heart. My refusal to give in to her demand for an opinion frustrated Evelyn. But it achieved our ultimate goal—it forced her back to herself, to the reality of her own fragile being. She was angry at me for it, but grateful at the same time.

In *Soulmaking*, Alan Jones writes:

> It is, perhaps, in the use and understanding of silence that the psychoanalytic and the desert [spiritual] traditions are most alike. Silence is important in all the great religious paths. It involves a kind of breakdown, an annihilation for the sake of reorganizing the way we perceive ourselves and the world. . . . Silence, in the end, can become a healing and comforting experience.

Silence in the therapeutic relationship provides a nonverbal space into which feelings can emerge. In Evelyn's case she felt ashamed when faced with her own sense of inadequacy and fear.

Again she lashed out at me, in an attempt to save herself from the pain she was feeling. "Tell me what you think! Why are you just sitting there torturing me? What's the point? Do you want to humiliate me? Well, you're doing a great job of it. I can't just sit here like this. I feel too ashamed. You must think I'm stupid and weak, not to be able to run my own life. Well, I am weak and stupid. I hate myself!" And tears poured out of her eyes.

At that point, I stepped in to comfort Evelyn by letting her know I wasn't trying to torture her, but that I understood how she was being tortured by her own inner conflict. There was a desperate need within her to depend upon someone seen as stronger or wiser. She felt unable to handle life's decisions alone; yet she saw how that dependence kept her trapped. As a means of developing her strength and confidence, I suggested to Evelyn that she make some minor "practice" decisions on her own. She agreed and, in the following week, was soon confronted with fear. One night, after making a practice decision, she called me in intense anxiety, saying, "I know I've made a mistake—it's just too awful—I can't bear it." She was sobbing on the line.

Finally finding the words to tell me what happened, it was true that Evelyn had made a mistake. It was a relatively minor one—but not to her. To Evelyn, there was no such thing as a small mistake. She was mortified and filled with self-hate and remorse. In this moment, her past conditioning revealed itself again. Having never had freedom of choice, she never had freedom to make mistakes either—never learning that mistakes are human, and part of the process of maturing and forming identity. Her parents had always presented themselves as all-knowing; they never appeared imperfect. No wonder she was afraid to try. Not only did she feel small and inadequate, but mistakes were unforgivable in her eyes!

Once again, I couldn't take away Evelyn's anguish, but my presence on the other end of the telephone line comforted her.

My interpretations helped give a perspective in the midst of the disproportionate shame and tragedy consuming her. Often, in therapy, people learn self-love and self-acceptance through the therapist's loving acceptance of them.

Evelyn continued in her practice decision-making and slowly worked through some of her fears. In the process, her attachment to her parents lessened, and her attachment to me grew. She started calling me more frequently and wanting to know details of my personal life. I was willing to answer some questions, but not others, instead choosing to explore the reasons for the questions.

"Well," she said, "I guess I want us to be friends. And I want to know that we're the same—that you have problems too, not just me."

Unlike Steven, who needed to be spared my problems, for Evelyn, knowledge of my humanness was very important and a welcome relief from the omniscient authority of her parents. But, while I could provide a model of authenticity for Evelyn, I could not be her friend in the way she wanted.

"Why not?" she demanded. The angry child in her felt entitled to whatever she asked for.

"Because it would interfere with the work we're doing together, that's why," I answered. "You came to me for help, and I think I can help you much more as a therapist than as a friend." Of course there is an element of friendship inherent in the therapeutic relationship. But what Evelyn was seeking was actually something else. She wanted to get away from her newborn feelings of independence—they were too threatening. She was unconsciously trying to recreate the same type of relationship she had with her parents—an enmeshed one, in which she could become absorbed, dissolve her identity, and be relieved of the burden of her individuality.

By setting limits, I was showing Evelyn responsibility to myself, as well as to her—affirming that we could be together, but also separate. Initially, she did not appreciate the lesson.

"You don't really like me at all," she said. "If you liked me, you wouldn't pull away. You think I'm a big baby and you can't wait to get away from me. Patricia never does that to me. We're always there for each other and can count on each other. That's why I love her."

To Evelyn, anything short of total fusion felt like abandonment. It was painful and confusing for her to redefine love. She had learned from her parents that overinvolvement is love and caring, and never includes separation or independence. Actually, overinvolvement *masquerades* as love, but is more about control; it fosters dependence while neglecting the child's need for freedom. Real love supports the child's need to become self-sufficient, not merely satisfying the parents' desires. Using the analogy of the bicycle: A child can begin learning to ride with the help of training wheels. Eventually though, the parents must take off the training wheels and let the child ride it alone—falls are inevitable, but sooner or later balance is found. If the parents can't tolerate their own fear, and can't trust the child's innate ability, the training wheels stay on and the child never enjoys the fun of riding a two-wheeler.

Little by little, Evelyn and I worked through her old beliefs. She came to understand that love and individuality are not mutually exclusive. As she gained confidence in herself, she began to relish her new freedom and was angry at her past limitations, and angry at her parents for holding her back. She challenged them with the truth about Patricia and stood for her decision to continue her career. Her parents did not react as catastrophically as she feared, but they were not happy. For several months, they broke all contact with Evelyn. She suffered greatly through this period, feeling the loss of her parents' approval. She said, "I guess I always knew in my heart that their love was conditional—as long as I was the daughter they wanted me to be, everything was fine. They just can't let me have my own life—and especially not gay. But I'm not willing to live for them anymore, it's just not worth it."

Becoming independent required Evelyn to learn more about herself. In subsequent sessions, we worked on clarifying her real values and desires. We also focused on her vulnerabilities, such as sensitivity to abandonment feelings. She needed to know her frailties, as well as her strengths, so she could take care of herself in difficult moments. Of course, she could still lean on others, but she also needed to be able to count on herself for comfort and support.

Evelyn and her parents slowly and tentatively began to reconnect, both sides fearful but hopeful. She was fortunate; sometimes reconciliations don't happen, or they take much longer to occur, and often they stay superficial and perfunctory.

As the time approached for Evelyn to leave therapy, one more old belief of hers came to the surface for healing.

"I feel so guilty and ashamed," she said. "After all you've done for me, how can I just walk out on you? I don't want to hurt your feelings. And besides, I know you think I shouldn't go, that I'm not 'cured' enough. I know you're thinking, 'Wait till she gets out there, she'll never make it.' You want me to stay, admit it—if for no other reason than because if I leave, you'll be losing money!"

It took several more sessions for us to work through this last issue. "You're afraid I'll be like your parents," I told Evelyn, "afraid I need you here for my benefit, and that I put my needs before yours." I mentioned before that Evelyn's parents rewarded her dependent behavior, and discouraged independence because of their fears she would not succeed on her own, or would not reflect the image they desired. There was also another reason—they had learned from *their* parents that love meant enmeshment. So, when in the natural course of her development Evelyn pulled away from them, *they* felt abandoned, and shamed her for doing something wrong. Now she was afraid I would feel the same, as she pulled away from me.

We were able to work through those fears firsthand, as she struggled for her freedom. "No, Evelyn," I said, "I don't think you are doing anything wrong. In fact, just the opposite. I believe you can make it. Yes, I'll miss you, and ending our relationship feels sad. But it also feels sweet because I see how much you've grown and changed. I am happy for you, and glad to have been a part of your progress."

Evelyn looked relieved. "Boy, that feels good. What a relief. I don't think I've ever had that kind of permission before. But are you sure?"

"Yes, I'm sure."

Her face suddenly darkened. "Well, I guess I'm out then. I just hope I can handle everything. What if . . ." She didn't finish her sentence, but I had a hunch about what Evelyn was thinking. She was in the old belief that as she finally stood up for herself and took independent action, she was going to be "disowned" by me and could never return.

I smiled and said, "You don't *have* to take care of everything alone. If you hit a rough spot in the road, you can always call me, or come back for as many sessions as you need. You haven't lost my support."

Her face brightened at this new option. "Really?" she said. "Great! Thanks!"

Her training wheels were off, and she was on her way.

The special relationship between client and therapist is renewed every time someone reaches out for help. The way the relationship can be used as an instrument for healing depends upon the skills and sensitivity of the therapist, the receptivity of the client, and the idiosyncrasies of both people's personalities. When all goes well, much good can come of it. As seen in the examples given, conditioned attitudes and reactions can be brought out for examination. Old pain can be expressed and released. People who have learned to be rigidly independent and mistrustful, or at the other extreme, overly dependent and self-effacing, can learn the flexibility of healthy intimacy. Solving problems of intimacy in human relations requires help. The very personal and dynamic interactions in psychotherapy provide a unique and effective opportunity for healing.

In *Between Therapist and Client*, Michael Kahn puts it like this:

> At the moment of the existential encounter between therapist and client, the client's whole world is present. All of the client's significant past relationships, all their most basic hopes and fears are there, and are focused upon the therapist. If we can make it possible for them to become aware of their world coming to rest in us, and if we can be there, fully there, to receive their awareness and respond to it, the relationship cannot help but become therapeutic.

CHAPTER 10

REBIRTH AND TRANSFORMATION: THE MYSTERY OF THERAPY

Growth and healing, because they are processes of nature, remain somewhat mysterious and can't be fully understood. During the healing of therapy, you will experience something analogous to the transformation of a caterpillar into a butterfly. The caterpillar lives its life on the ground, apparently knowing nothing else. One day it finds a little niche and begins to spin a cocoon around itself. What happens in the darkness of the cocoon? Is the caterpillar frightened? Does it feel pain as it goes through changes inside its temporary home? Does it feel a death of its former self? Does it know its future? All we know for sure is that it gradually becomes something quite different from what it was before; it grows beautiful wings and, eventually, breaks out of a shell that has become too small.

The cocoon of therapy can also feel dark and cramped at times, with no future in sight—but all the while the psyche within is transforming. The death of the old self, metaphorically speaking, is necessary for the new self to be born. Our reluctance to "fall apart" is based on our shortsighted caterpillar-like point of view. We fear going into the cocoon, because we don't know we are to become butterflies. Taking the step into therapy is an act of courage—it is a step taken, not without fear, but in spite of it.

Because the transformation is not easy, many people drop out along the way. In *The Road Less Traveled*, Scott Peck talks about those people who *do* have the courage to begin, and to follow through in therapy. He says they

> . . . find themselves not only cured and free from the curses of their childhood and ancestry but also find themselves living in a new and different world. What they once perceived as problems they now perceive as opportunities. What were once loathsome barriers are now welcome challenges. Thoughts previously unwanted become helpful insights; feelings previously disowned become sources of energy and guidance. Occurrences that once seemed to be burdens now seem to be gifts.

This new and different world reveals itself bit by bit; the rebirth happens gradually, imperceptibly most of the time. You might observe something suddenly—a change in attitude, a different response to a familiar event, a new feeling about yourself.

One man, toward the end of his therapy, remarked, "Things are changing—or maybe *things* aren't changing but *I'm* changing. I'm noticing wonderful things I didn't notice before, and feeling things I didn't feel before." His comments reflect a lightness many people describe, a lightness that is a result of throwing off the burden of unresolved problems. Without the weight of emotional pain lingering from the past, you are freer to experience life's sounds, sights, new activities, new people. Without the obsessional, inward focus caused by emotional turmoil, you are freer to look outward.

A quote from T. S. Eliot describes this rejuvenation in "Little Gidding" of *Four Quartets*:

> *We shall not cease from exploration*
> *And the end of all our exploring*
> *Will be to arrive where we started*
> *And know the place for the first time.*

Each "mini-rebirth" arises spontaneously, often after the resolution of a difficult emotional struggle in therapy, or after the grieving of an old wound. Each positive growth experience builds on the last, contributing to the gradual reshaping of personality.

Rhonda made a lot of progress in her first months of therapy. She had been tormented by anxiety, especially in social situations. One day, after many sessions of working through the sources of her anxiety, she came in smiling, and said, "Last night I went to a party. It was the kind of party I would have given anything to avoid a few months ago. But this time I forced myself, because I'm trying not to give in to my fear anymore. On the way over, I was nervous, but when the hostess greeted me, I relaxed. Next thing I knew, it was two hours later and I had been *talking* to people the whole time. Amazing—I wasn't off by myself like I usually would be. And I wasn't looking suspiciously at everyone, judging them, and worrying about what they were saying. I used to be so sure they were talking about me. What a laugh. Last night I realized they were all much too absorbed in their own good time to be thinking about me."

Rhonda experienced a moment of rebirth at that party. Suddenly she saw her new self behaving differently—at ease, feeling secure, and enjoying the evening. This gave her the opportunity to measure her progress. Until then, she didn't really know that some of her anxiety was healed. Naturally she was elated, and motivated to continue her work with me.

A few weeks later, however, she came into my office despondent, saying, "It's hopeless. I thought I was getting better, but now I feel like it's back to square one."

"What happened?" I asked.

"My car broke down and I had to take a bus to work. The bus stop was so crowded; people were all over the place. I just couldn't handle it. First I moved away from the bench and stood by myself, but it still seemed like some of them were staring at me. Finally I got so anxious—I knew it would be worse on the bus, so I gave up, walked to a phone booth and called a cab. I'm so depressed. How could this have happened? I was doing so well."

"You *are* doing well," I reassured her. "This was an unusual situation, something out of the norm for you. When was the last time you rode a bus?"

"I can't remember. Maybe a year ago."

"Okay, that's my point. You've become much less anxious in your everyday life. Circumstances that used to frighten you a lot have now become nonthreatening, right?"

"Right," she answered, still looking desperate but with a little hope in her voice.

"But, when you're hit with an extraordinary occurrence, like the bus stop, especially coupled with an upset like a car problem, what you get is a major stressor. And in times of great stress, we're all at our worst. It's natural to react in an old, habitual way. That doesn't mean you're back at square one. It may feel as bad, but you're only there temporarily—you haven't lost all the progress you've made."

Momentary setbacks during therapy are normal for everyone. Though you feel as if you are losing ground, it is not so. Whatever emotional growth you've achieved cannot be taken away. But the road to health is not straight and smooth; it winds, curves, goes up and down, and has plenty of bumps. Sometimes it goes back in the direction it came, and other times it seems to go in circles. Nevertheless it moves inexorably forward in time and space. You can never be in the same place twice.

Rhonda seemed comforted by my words. Other progressions in therapy had taught her that when she felt defeated, as if she were in a breakdown, a surge of emotional growth usually followed. But now these apparent "regressions" shook her faith; she didn't expect them to happen anymore. Part of transformation is learning to be less fearful when things don't go the way we expect them to, or think they should go. Attempting to control life is a fear-based behavior. Yes, we can take action in the directions we want to go, but we also must be flexible, open to life's influences and demands. Surrendering some control requires trust, both in self and in life. If you believe in yourself, you know you will be all right, even if events around you are not going according to your plan. Surrender is humbling, but not humiliating. We are humiliated when we base our life upon the narrow vision of our egos. We set ourselves up by believing we have total control; then, when we fail, naturally we feel victimized. Surrender does not mean resigning ourselves to the smallness of being human; rather, it is embracing the larger whole, of which we are a part.

On the other hand, trusting life and surrendering to it doesn't mean all goes well. Not at all. What trusting does mean is accepting difficult as well as easy times—not without pain, but with less self-pity and bitterness. It means finding what was gained, what lesson learned, even from the apparently most unfair and miserable circumstances. The advantage of this attitude, contrary to resignation, is a much more positive, harmonious, grateful, and even joyful experience of events that from an earlier perspective would have appeared negative.

Along with acceptance of self and life comes the capacity for compassion. The birth of compassion in a person's soul is a moving thing to witness. Some people are able to have compassion for others but not for themselves. Then there are those who must find self-love *before* they are capable of empathy for another.

Jeffrey, a man who was always extremely exacting with himself and others, described his change like this: "My father taught me to be a taskmaster. I used to constantly be on my own case so bad I got ulcers. After that, I knew I had to do something different, but what did I do? I started exercising to reduce stress, and found out the more exercise I did, the more strength and endurance I had. Great! Know what I used my new strength and endurance for? To work more! I got so compulsive about work and exercise that I had a heart attack. Isn't that ridiculous? I was relentless with my employees, too—drove those guys into the ground. The weirdest part of all was that I thought it was the right thing—I told myself my standards were high and that I demanded excellence of everyone. I even thought my employees should have thanked me for pushing them to do their best. When they didn't thank me, but were resentful instead, I called them ungrateful. Now that I've gotten a different perspective, I see why they resented me. I said I cared about them and that's why I wanted them to do well, but I never once asked them what they needed or how they felt. I was just on my own ego trip.

"Same with my wife. She used to get mad at me whenever I teased her. I liked teasing her, thought it was fun. The more I teased, the more upset she got; the more upset she got, the more fun I had. I thought it was all a great game—didn't see her side at all. The game wasn't fun for her. It took having both of us here, in a therapy session, for me to really listen, to hear that she was hurting. I was teasing her about areas where she already felt insecure, or self-conscious. My attitude was, 'Get over it!' I had no patience for anyone's frailties, including my own. It just wasn't acceptable to me to be weak, slow, tired, vulnerable—anything but perfect all the time. No wonder I got ulcers and had a heart attack. Now I'm a lot easier on myself and the people around me. I don't have to be perfect to be good enough. And I can slow down and care enough to understand someone else's point of view."

Jeffrey had changed, remarkably. He even looked different from before. His face, which used to be furrowed into a permanent frown, had relaxed and softened. He let his hair grow just a bit, and wore it in a looser style. When he started therapy, he always wore a suit and tie; gradually he began loosening the tie, then leaving it off altogether. Eventually he showed up in casual clothes. External changes like Jeffrey's are common—they are simply outer manifestations of an inner shift. Jeffrey became more self-loving through his therapy. Most people do. Understanding the sources of our frailties makes them easier to bear. Grieving the emotional wounds of the past lessens their hold. Since shame traps us in our emotional prisons of fear and self-hate, the healing of shame frees us to be simply who we are. Realizing the truth of who we are, both strengths as well as weaknesses, we change what we can, and accept what can't be changed as lovingly as possible.

One woman said, "Now I don't feel like there's something wrong with me for having problems—I know other people do, too. I still feel lonely and I hurt sometimes, but I don't feel ashamed about it anymore. We all have disabilities—some of them you can see, some of them you can't."

Becoming more self-loving also means learning to see the strengths *within* the weaknesses. Jeffrey's perfectionism, once moderated, was no longer a threat to his life but instead became a contribution to it. He was able to be thorough and efficient in his work, to recognize in others the heartless taskmaster he once had been, and have compassion for them. By understanding his own and other people's behavior better, he became kinder and not always subject to compulsive actions and reactions. He dropped his sarcastic teasing, but kept a keen and witty sense of humor.

Even beyond self-acceptance and compassion, we can come to see our vulnerabilities as opportunities for growth. When we follow our pain to its source, we heal wounds of the past, and we find ourselves altered in the process, pointed in new directions previously undiscovered.

In 12-Step recovery meetings, people sometimes say they are grateful to be addicts or alcoholics. This means that only through the downfall brought on by their addictions did they find themselves reoriented to a more spiritual life, a life they would never have found otherwise.

Dr. Gerald May, in *Addiction and Grace*, says:

> We can think of our inadequacies as terrible defects, if we want, and hate ourselves. But we can also think of them affirmatively, as doorways through which the power of grace can enter our lives.

I believe that psychological transformation at its best is a spiritual transformation as well. Through the doorways of your pain and struggle, unforeseen and glorious changes can enter, changes that you never expected, in your desire to solve problems and feel better. Yes, you can solve problems and feel better, but you can have more than that.

Elizabeth Barrett Browning says it well in her *Sonnets from the Portuguese*: "God's gifts put man's best dreams to shame." In other words, we are limited by our own limited beliefs and lack of imagination.

Shelley, a woman who worked with me for several years, summed up the changes she had gone through: "All my life I have been trying to make up for my childhood. I grew up an only child, and we were poor. We weren't just poor financially, we were poor in every way. My mother was a small, self-effacing soul who never had anything, and never expected anything. She always played the martyr. Actually, she wasn't playing—she felt like life's victim. But she never tried to make anything better. My father earned just enough money for us to scrape by, and my mother took care of me and the house. She'd always say things like, 'Don't worry, honey, we'll make do.' I hated that, especially as a teenager. Why not more? I grew up believing that the most I could hope for was to 'make do.' In my adult life, I tried to compensate by earning lots of money and living extravagantly—always trying to prove to the world how well I was doing. Now I realize I was still carrying around that old attitude from home. My job, my friends, my love relationships—nothing was ever the way I *really* wanted it. I was in control when it came to money—I had plenty of it—but emotionally I still lived in the scarcity economy of my childhood, never happy, just making do. I was angry inside all the time, feeling like things were never right.

"Being here helped me realize I was stuck in the past, even though I was fighting it. I guess I had to let myself feel all the misery I was carrying around, before I could get past it. It was tough to admit how angry I was at my mother for being so resigned. It's not easy to get angry at martyrs; they seem to try so hard and they're so pitiful.

"I guess it's true that you keep re-creating the past until you deal with it. I don't have to do that anymore."

Shelley's belief in scarcity is probably the most common belief that hinders people from taking advantage of opportunities to enhance their lives. It also stops people from *creating* opportunities. Beliefs like "What I want just isn't available" or "What I'm looking for is available, but not to me" are self-defeating and very often untrue. They stem from a time in the past when they *were* true however. In many families love and/or money just aren't available, or are given only in small quantities. From those situations we derive a system of negative ideas that, if unquestioned, are carried with us the rest of our lives.

As you let go of outworn beliefs, you can affirm new ones: Love *is* in abundance. There *is* enough to go around. It *is* okay to desire love, to have love, to enjoy love.

A principle of metaphysical philosophy is that you can have only what you believe is possible. You attract to yourself people and circumstances that reflect your vision of life; your life is determined by your beliefs about it. We can't know if this is true, any more than we can know the truth of any philosophy, but the message is a positive one: Change your beliefs and you can change your life. Having affirmative beliefs doesn't eliminate all problems, but at least you no longer have to get in the way of your own success.

Shelley said more about the changes she experienced: "Besides believing I can have more, I also feel differently about what I *don't* have. Before, whenever anything didn't go my way, I was furious. You'd think the world was coming to an end by the way I acted—yelling and crying and carrying on. But for me the world *had* ended. Every time I was deprived of anything, I fell right back into the pit of my deprived childhood. I felt like the poorest, saddest little girl—and the angriest. Why should *I*, the financially powerful adult, have to be deprived for even one minute? Without realizing it, I had become a martyr just like my mother—a long-suffering victim—only I was louder than she was. Now, after working through all the old pain, I don't fall into that pit so often, and when I do, I get out faster. I can take better care of myself. I feel stronger, more able to tolerate pain when I have to. And instead of giving myself pessimistic, victim messages when I'm down, I say positive helpful things like, 'You'll be okay. It's not forever!' I remind myself that even though I may *feel* like a deprived child sometimes, I'm really not. Everyone suffers, not only me. I don't compare my suffering to other people's as much as before. I know that some things will go my way, some won't. I'm not as attached to having my way as I used to be, because I've seen that when I get what I want, it doesn't always turn out for the best. When I'm open to what life brings, sometimes I'm surprised at how good it can be.

"Just last weekend, someone offered to take me river-rafting. Now, I had never been river-rafting, but my attitude in the past was that it was just a silly trend and I wanted no part of it. All that splashing and screaming, and being crowded together with other people, sounded way too close for me. But this time, for some reason, I felt like breaking out of my usual mold, letting myself try something different. When the day came, I realized I was more scared of the danger than anything else, but I went ahead with it anyway. And you know what? I had a *great* time! I laughed and screamed with the rest of them—fell in the water and climbed back on the raft. I couldn't believe it was me. I loved it!"

It's heartwarming to hear clients talk about how therapy has helped them. I like hearing accounts of new behaviors replacing old ones, confidence appearing where there was none before, feelings of relief from depression and anxiety. It's good to be told stories of people with renewed motivation and courage, venturing out to try something different. Sometimes the visible changes are big ones—recovery from addiction or codependence, a new career direction, a marriage, an overdue divorce. Sometimes they are smaller but still significant—beginning a creative hobby, a sport, taking a vacation. I love watching people blossom from fearful buds into wide-open flowers eager to feel the sun.

In addition to changes within individuals, another significant transformation is in the area of communication. We're communicating all the time, in one way or another. But in order to speak our minds and hearts, to express feelings, to defend ourselves and resolve conflicts, we need to know how to communicate *well*.

When I was a child, and my brother and I had a fight, my mother would tell us never to go to sleep mad at each other. We had to apologize first and make up. That seemed like a pretty good idea at the time, except when *I* wasn't ready to apologize, or didn't feel I had anything to be sorry about. I still think resolving conflicts right away is the best idea, if possible. As children, though, my brother and I didn't have the ability to resolve our differences, so we just patched things up. Today we do have that ability; it makes a difference.

Most adults never learned how to express feelings and thoughts in direct, nonabusive ways. Yet, what other skill is more important in relationships? Wouldn't it be a relief to be able to *say* you're angry, rather than stomping around and slamming doors? And wouldn't it feel better to express pain and sadness in words, instead of pouting and getting depressed? The skills of communication are priceless. Without them we get lost in a painful tangle of manipulative words, fearfully circling the subject at hand. Or, just as painfully, we tear each other apart, through ever-escalating arguments laced with insults, yelling across rooms, out of control.

Without effective communication there's no hope for resolution of conflict. We may stop fighting, pretending to forget the problems, but chronic undercurrents of hurt and hostility linger and build, poisoning relationships. Spiteful actions, seemingly out of nowhere, then speak from the undercurrents.

Reversing bad communication patterns is possible, and not very difficult. With a little education and practice, much is accomplished. We can't always make up before bedtime, but we can certainly do our best to keep relationships healthier by keeping communication clear.

Betty and Earl, a couple I spoke about earlier, were very pleased with the changes between them. Betty said, "I'm not as afraid of Earl as I used to be, since I worked through all that fear of my father. It's definitely easier to deal with the present when past stuff doesn't take over so much. And besides, since we both know now how sensitive I am to anger, I can take responsibility for my overreactions when they do happen."

Earl jumped in: "I'm not as afraid and ashamed of feelings in general as I used to be, and I don't feel so guilty about having them, either. It helps that Betty's not always pointing the finger at me, like I'm the bad guy."

Betty answered, "Yeah, that's probably the biggest breakthrough for me. Coming from a family of arguers, I've always wanted to win—one person had to be right and the other wrong. Of course I was usually right." She smiled, continuing, "Since, as a child, I was so afraid of my father's abusive rages, I took another tack—shaming, blaming, and manipulating. There was never a middle ground. Now I know how to say to Earl, 'I feel angry' or 'I feel hurt,' instead of '*You* did this' and 'You *always* do that.' "

Earl, looking pleased, said, "It's definitely better for me. All that blaming just pushed me away and gave me a good excuse to stay shut down."

Betty went on, "Finally I see that there isn't always a right and a wrong, that it's just two points of view. And it's much better to try to understand each other's point of view than to win. 'Cause when one wins, one loses. And when that happens, we both lose, because we're pulled apart. Understanding is a better goal—it brings us together. But it took a while to let go of the old way. It helped when I heard someone say, 'Would you rather be happy or right?' I'd rather be happy."

The changes brought about in therapy are as numerous and varied as the people benefiting from them. Every person's transformation is a remarkable blend of needs, history, and personality. What actually makes the changes occur is also a blend—of talking, remembering, feeling, believing, understanding, sharing, caring and, above all, the mysterious element of healing. I have described the mental, emotional, and behavioral aspects of therapy, but in my opinion the key ingredient of change is still incomprehensible, because it is the spiritual essence of life, responsible for all growth and healing.

To understand the therapy process fully, you have to experience it firsthand. And when you do, don't be surprised if what you find is more than what you sought. Therapy not only helps you resolve past and current problems but also shows you your personal history and pain in a different way. They are not the enemies they once were, not something to be overcome once and for all, but instead, a part of your life story, which has given you compassion, humility, and an orientation toward growth and self-actualization.

To accept yourself with your imperfections and vulnerabilities is, at the same time, to accept life on its own terms—to be willing to go *through* pain instead of fighting it or running from it, and to look for lessons and silver linings instead of seeing only clouds. Acceptance is also knowing that sometimes, in spite of all your courage and best intentions, you'll be lost in the clouds anyway—that life does include pain, injustice, and despair beyond our understanding.

As you evolve, people will see the difference in you, and comment on how you've changed. "You're calmer, more grounded," they'll say. Or, "You're not as angry as you used to be, or as sad. You seem less preoccupied—happier, lighter."

Healing emotionally frees you to be more of who you want to be, and to do more of what you want to do. It can open your eyes and heart to a whole new way of seeing or being, and of relating to others. Less fearful, with more faith in yourself and life, you'll have a greater capacity for meaningful activities and intimate relationships. You come to trust, through experience, that many events that seem like mistakes or disappointments at the time of their occurrence, actually work for your good in the long run. Sometimes the wisest action is no action at all, and some lessons are learned only through suffering.

Above all, healing emotionally gives you a deeper, more loving, harmonious, and spiritual relationship with yourself. You are more conscious, more aware of everything; your intuition guides you. Initially, this new consciousness is a bit disconcerting.

In *The Road Less Traveled*, Scott Peck writes:

> When we are given a new vision of ourselves, and of the world, we are pushed deeper and deeper into solitude.

> Perhaps that is why so many of us are resistant to spiritual growth. The threat of solitude frightens us.

The solitude Dr. Peck refers to is not the loneliness of isolation, not the prison of shame and emotional pain—quite the opposite. It's a place where you meet yourself free of masks; where you touch the spiritual skin of life, taste its flavor, and breathe its breath. No longer needing to run away from, or toward, anything, you stand still in the fullness of life. But the fullness is also an emptiness—not an emptiness that needs to be filled, not the emptiness of depression and apathy. It's the emptying out of old conflicts that used to clutter up your inner world, noisily drowning out any hope of silence. The space is now empty, quiet, a place in which you are alone and not alone at the same time. What's frightening about solitude is its mystery. But just like solitude, silence can be frightening too, an unfamiliar texture to the fabric of the moment. Peaceful and exciting, it is both a void and a presence. It contains nothing and everything.

In *Soulmaking*, Alan Jones says:

> For the believer this terrible inner absence, while never ceasing to have something awesome about it, is gradually perceived as a gift. Slowly in the life of faith, the thing that we dread becomes both companion and friend.
>
> To the believer, this vast inner emptiness is nothing less than the dwelling place of God.

When your relationship with yourself is healed, solitude and silence can be appreciated as pathways to the soul. A transformation has indeed occurred, and all aspects of your life reflect it.

LOOKING BACK

> The healing of the spirit
> has not been completed
> until openness to challenge
> becomes a way of life.
> —M. Scott Peck
> *The Road Less Traveled*

Psychotherapy touches not only the mind and emotions, but also the spirit. As the mind and emotions heal, the spirit heals, too. This healing process is a journey chosen by relatively few people. If you are one of those, credit yourself as courageous, wise, and fortunate. You'll never regret the choice. The beginning might be frightening and arduous, but it gets easier as you go along. However, once you've begun, once you're fully on the road, there's no turning back. You might stop to rest occasionally, or even decide to get off the road altogether, but you can never return to the place of not knowing, to the unconsciousness of earlier days. Sometimes you may wish you *could* return, because the journey gets painful and the old days seem simpler in your memory. But you can't go back, and even if you could, ultimately you wouldn't choose to. It's like having been blind all your life, and suddenly you're able to see: movement, colors, and shapes pour in, more than you even imagined. Much of what fills your vision is beautiful and miraculous, but ugliness enters in too, uninvited, along with the grotesque and horrifying. You don't like everything in life's mixture of joy and pain, yet having experienced it, you wouldn't want to go back to blindness. And even if you cover your eyes, you can never forget what you've seen.

Psychotherapy will help to free you from old pain, the suffering caused by your unresolved past. You can *lessen* pain still more by not resisting it—accepting suffering, when it comes, as a part of life. Your *idea* of suffering will be modified if you look for the lessons it holds. But no amount of therapy can completely solve the problem of pain. In spite of our longing for total, constant joy and freedom, peace, and satisfaction, it is apparently not in the nature of human life to reach that ideal. Nevertheless, our longings persist. This paradoxical longing and striving for an unattainable goal is also in the nature of life. Spurred on, sometimes by pleasure, at other times by pain, we continue to strive, and, if our minds and hearts are open, we learn from our striving.

Dr. Gerald May, in *Addiction and Grace*, writes:

> Authentic spiritual wholeness, by its very nature, is open-ended. It is always in the process of becoming, always incomplete. . . .
>
> Our fundamental dis-ease, then . . . is not a sign of something wrong, but of something more profoundly right than we could ever dream of. . . . It is God's song of love in our soul.

The healing of emotional pain leads us to a deeper relationship with ourselves. Just as pain has been our guide to healing, our spiritual restlessness, or "dis-ease," is a guide to the spiritual dimension of life. It is a voice reminding us of something beyond.

Our *process of becoming* never ends, but that doesn't mean therapy never ends. Therapy comes to a close when you've resolved, to your satisfaction, current problems and past traumas. Then old patterns can be recognized and dealt with as they occur, or can be avoided altogether. It ends when you can fully allow and express feelings—when you've begun to love and accept yourself and life, and to love others in a healthy way, knowing also that you never stop learning how to love. You're ready to leave therapy when you understand yourself emotionally, and, with that understanding and love, can help yourself through difficult times. Trusting yourself, you are led to a more faith-full experience of life. You gravitate more enthusiastically toward what is good, as a plant grows toward the light. With trust and faith, you are freer to risk, to stretch the limits of who you are and what you do.

Even though therapy ends, growth continues. When psychological problems become less pressing, larger issues of life come into focus. Whether inside or outside the context of therapy, questions of meaning, identity, choice, love, pain, death, and God ask to be answered. The journey of self-knowledge, and spiritual and emotional growth, goes on.

If you would like to contact the author,
you may do so by writing to:

JOYCE HOUSER WARD, M.F.C.T.
610 Santa Monica Blvd Suite 214
Santa Monica, CA 90401

BIBLIOGRAPHY

Alcoholics Anonymous. New York: Alcoholics Anonymous World Wide Services, Inc., 1976.

Bass, Ellen, and Laura Davis. *The Courage to Heal: A Guide for Women Survivors of Child Sexual Abuse*. New York: Harper & Row, 1988.

Beattie, Melody. *Beyond Codependency and Getting Better All the Time*. San Francisco: Harper & Row, 1989.

Bradshaw, John. *Bradshaw On: The Family—A Revolutionary Way of Self-Discovery*. Deerfield Beach, FL: Health Communications, Inc., 1988.

———. *Healing the Shame That Binds You*. Deerfield Beach, FL: Health Communications, Inc., 1988.

Covington, Stephanie, and Liana Beckett. *Leaving the Enchanted Forest: The Path From Relationship Addiction to Intimacy*. San Francisco: Harper & Row, 1988.

Firestone, Robert W., *The Fantasy Bond: Effects of Psychological Defenses on Interpersonal Relations.* New York: Human Sciences Press, Inc., 1987.

Goldstein, Joseph, and Jack Kornfield. *Seeking the Heart of Wisdom: The Path of Insight Meditation.* Boston: Shambhala Publications, Inc., 1987.

Gorski, Terence T. *The Players and Their Personalities: Understanding People Who Get Involved in Addictive Relationships.* Independence, MO: Herald House/Independence Press, 1989.

Hedges, Lawrence E. *Listening Perspectives in Psychotherapy.* Northvale, NJ: Jason Aronson, 1983.

Hillman, James. *Re-Visioning Psychology.* New York: Harper & Row, 1975.

Jacoby, Mario. *The Analytic Encounter: Transference and Human Relationship.* Toronto: Inner City Books, 1984.

Jones, Alan.*Exploring Spiritual Direction: An Essay on Christian Friendship.* San Francisco: Harper & Row, 1982.

———. *Soulmaking: The Desert Way of Spirituality.* San Francisco: Harper & Row, 1985.

Kahn, Michael. *Between Therapist and Client: The New Relationship.* New York: W. H. Freeman and Company, 1991.

Kaufman, Gershen. *Shame: The Power of Caring.* Rochester, VT: Schenkman Books, Inc., 1980, 1985.

Laing, R. D. *The Divided Self.* Harmondsworth, Middlesex, UK: Pelican Books, 1969.

Larsen, Earnie. *Stage II Recovery: Life Beyond Addiction.* San Francisco: Harper & Row, 1985.

Leonard, Linda Schierse. *Witness to the Fire: Creativity and the Veil of Addiction.* Boston: Shambhala Publications, Inc., 1989.

Lerner, Michael. *Surplus Powerlessness.* Oakland: The Institute for Labor and Mental Health, 1986. Available through *Tikkun* magazine, 5100 Leona Street, Oakland, CA 94619.

Mahler, Margaret S., Fred Pine, and Anni Bergman. *The Psychological Birth of the Human Infant*. New York: Basic Books, 1975.

May, Gerald G. *Addiction and Grace*. San Francisco: Harper & Row, 1988.

Mellody, Pia. *Facing Codependence*. San Francisco: Harper & Row, 1989.

Miller, Alice. *For Your Own Good: Hidden Cruelty in Child-Rearing and the Roots of Violence*. New York: Farrar, Straus and Giroux, 1983.

———. *The Drama of the Gifted Child: How Narcissistic Parents Form and Deform the Emotional Lives of Their Talented Children*. New York: Basic Books, 1981.

———. *Thou Shalt Not Be Aware: Society's Betrayal of the Child*. New York: Farrar, Straus and Giroux, 1984.

Norwood, Robin. *Women Who Love Too Much: When You Keep Wishing and Hoping He'll Change*. Los Angeles: Jeremy Tarcher, 1985.

Oliver-Diaz, Philip, and Patricia A. O'Gorman. *12-Steps to Self-Parenting*. Deerfield Beach, FL: Health Communications, Inc., 1988.

Paulus, Trina. *Hope for the Flowers*. New York: Paulist Press, 1972.

Peck, M. Scott, M.D. *The Road Less Traveled: A New Psychology of Love, Traditional Values and Spiritual Growth*. New York: Simon & Schuster, 1978.

Pollard, John K. III. *Self-Parenting: The Complete Guide to Your Inner Conversations*. Malibu, CA: Generic Human Studies Publishing, 1987.

Scarf, Maggie. *Intimate Partners: Patterns in Love and Marriage*. New York: Random House, 1987.

Schaef, Anne Wilson. *Escape from Intimacy: Untangling the "Love" Addictions: Sex, Romance, Relationships.* San Francisco: Harper & Row, 1989.

Sex and Love Addicts Anonymous. Boston: The Augustine Fellowship, Sex and Love Addicts Anonymous Fellowship-Wide Services, Inc., 1986.

Whitfield, Charles L. *Healing the Child Within: Discovery and Recovery for Adult Children of Dysfunctional Families.* Deerfield Beach, FL: Health Communications, Inc., 1987.

Wolf, Ernest S. *Treating the Self: Elements of Clinical Self-Psychology.* New York: The Guilford Press, 1988.